East comes West

KU-367-908

a background to some Asian faiths

by PEGGY HOLROYDE
in collaboration with MOHAMMED IQBAL
and DHARAM KUMAR VOHRA

foreword by LORD WADE
*President, Yorkshire Committee for
Community Relations*

Community Relations Commission
Russell Square House Russell Square London WC1

NOTES ON AUTHORS

Mrs PEGGY HOLROYDE, B.A.

Radcliffe College, Harvard University. Studied Eastern Religions under Dr. Radhakrishnan at Oxford. Lived in India 1953-58 and travelled to Pakistan. Lectures on Hinduism and Asian culture at Oversea Service College, Farnham Castle, Surrey. Leeds member, Yorkshire Committee Community Relations. Convener of YCCR Religious and Cultural Panel.

Mr MOHAMMED IQBAL, M.Sc.

Punjab University, M.Phil., London. Five years teaching experience at Huddersfield Spring Grove C. P. School. W.E.A. lecturer on Asian faiths, and in Urdu. One-time Vice-Chairman, Liaison Committee and founder of 'Home-Tutor Scheme' teaching Asian ladies English in Huddersfield. Member from Huddersfield of YCCR. Research scholar for Ph.D. at Huddersfield Polytechnic.

Mr DHARAM KUMAR VOHRA, B.A. (Hons.)

Punjab University, M.A., Punjab University. Specialist in Hindi, Urdu and Sanskrit languages. Court interpreter, Lecturer in Urdu, Bradford Technica College and Police Liaison Officer, Bradford City Police. Bradford member YCCR.

FOREWORD

by

Lord Wade, D.L., M.A., LL.B.,
Chairman of the Yorkshire Committee for Community Relations

I commend this booklet not only for the wealth of information that it provides but also for the better understanding which it is designed to achieve. There are many potential causes of misunderstanding in Britain today, that have nothing to do with racial prejudice. Some who come to this country, after leaving behind the warm hospitality of the East, get the impression that British people are aloof and this aloofness is sometimes mistaken for racism.

We, on our part, who live in a comparatively sophisticated urban society do not always appreciate how different life is here from the predominantly village society of India or Pakistan. We do not make sufficient allowances for the magnitude of the change. Another and even greater cause for misunderstanding is the failure to appreciate the part which religion plays in the lives of those who come from Asian countries, where social customs spring from centuries of religious tradition. Art, music, food, dress and the whole attitude to life is influenced by religion – considerably more so than in Western society.

The purpose of this booklet is not to make converts, still less to express value judgments, but to provide information and thereby lessen misunderstandings and embarrassments. Most of us are very ignorant of other people's faiths; yet, in areas such as the West Riding of Yorkshire, where there is a substantial number of Asian settlements, the need for more information to assist principals of colleges, teachers, social welfare workers and many others is undeniable. For example, a domestic science teacher may find herself with a class of thirteen-year-olds, one-third of whom may be Pakistani or Indian, another third West Indian and the rest native British. Some of these girls will be unwilling to cook or eat a sausage or a pork chop, while others will refuse to handle a beef stew or the conventional roast beef of old England. A teacher who has never encountered this situation may become impatient.

There are other factors that have arisen which require adequate explanations for head teachers, home visitors such as midwives, volunteers teaching English to Asian women, police, factory managers and trades union leaders.

In industry it is essential to explain why Muslim workers so often ask for Eid holiday at the last minute due to the problem of 'the siting and the sighting of the moon'. Managers may be willing to give holidays to meet their employees' convenience where mills are run with a predominance of Pakistani labour, but they like to have notice in advance in order to organise production. Again,

5

midwives want to know why a baby has to be shaved at birth, teachers are puzzled by the controversy over shalwar-kameez or over Sikh boys and girls being allowed to wear the kara around their wrists when West Indian girls say 'Please Miss, why can't I wear my bangles?' All these questions have to be answered sympathetically and intelligently. Then there is the problem facing the school staff when children are shy of mixed swimming or of taking off clothes for the gymnasium. Sometimes children are inclined to utter the word 'religion' as an excuse for getting out of any activity they do not like. If teachers are to meet these difficulties they must be accurately informed. Goodwill, though essential, is not by itself enough.

To meet this need for information the Religious and Cultural Panel of the Yorkshire Committee for Community Relations set to work, under the able chairmanship of Mrs Peggy Holroyde, to produce an account of Asian Faiths, Cultures and Social Customs. The West Indians, with their strong Christian tradition did not come within the scope of this study, but the Panel itself is very broadly based. It includes a number of Muslim, Hindu, Sikh and Christian representatives. It includes a Methodist Minister who is chairman of the International Committee in Keighley, a Quaker who teaches in Huddersfield, a Jamaican Presbyterian Deaconess, a Pakistani woman social welfare worker in Sheffield, the Secretary of the Yorkshire YMCAs, a Jewish adviser and a West Indian preacher of fundamentalist outlook.

Despite the differences of religious background, the members of the Panel have worked together harmoniously for three years, providing speakers for Conferences, encouraging local radio and TV stations to think of their immigrant listeners and viewers, advising British groups who wish to know more about the religions of immigrant communities and above all striving to win the battle against ignorance. It was appropriate that such a group should undertake the task of promoting this booklet.

The Yorkshire Committee owes a debt of gratitude to Mrs Peggy Holroyde, without whose energy and enthusiasm the report could never have been produced, and to Mr Iqbal and Mr Vohra who have given so painstakingly of their time and help. In thanking them I wish at the same time to express my gratitude to all those of the Sikh, Hindu and Muslim faiths in Yorkshire who have helped to ensure that the factual information is accurate. The manuscripts have been carefully studied by those who know their subjects well and their favourable comments have been most encouraging.

Finally, I wish to express the thanks of the Yorkshire Committee to the Community Relations Commission for undertaking the publication of this report. I am sure that those who read it will agree that the work of the panel has been worthwhile.

HINDUISM

by

**Dharam Kumar Vohra and
Peggy Holroyde**

The word Hinduism stands for the faith of the Hindus, approximately 500 million of its followers being inhabitants of India. The word Hindu is not to be found in any Sanskrit, Pali, Prakrit or other semi-classical language dictionary. It is derived from a corrupted form of the word 'Sindhu' which is the Sanskrit name of the river Indus in that part of the sub-continent where the Aryan migratory tribes first settled over 4,000 years ago.

There are many Sanskrit words beginning with this 'S' sound which, when spoken in Persian, or Urdu, lose the sound of the 'S' and adopt the sound of 'H'. The Sanskrit words 'Saptah' and 'Sapt' which mean week and seven respectively, are spoken as 'Haptah' and 'Haft' in Persian.

The Indus Valley Civilisation and Aryan Thought

Somewhere around 2500-2000 BC the Aryans came to the Indian sub-continent through Persia and the high passes of Asia Minor, so giving the modern countries of Pakistan and India a common historical background of at least 45 centuries of recorded history.

This wandering resilient people who spread from the central steppes of Eastern Europe, and left their racial memory in the minds of most white Europeans up to the Arctic circle of Iceland and Sweden (Sverige, the word used by Swedish people for their own country, has common roots with the Sanskrit word Svurg meaning Heaven), have, in a sense, made the darker-skinned races of the Indian sub-continent our blood brothers. Indeed we have a common ancestry in our common Aryan progenitors.

But the Aryans, for long held as the creators of Indian civilisation, are not now regarded as such. Recent excavations of the Indus Valley civilisation by such well-known TV personalities as Sir Mortimer Wheeler, have begun to discover at a deeper level of digging, certain terracotta figurines and medallions (one in Yogic Asana or posture) which indicate that the strongly ascetic tradition which we all recognise as characteristic of Indian thought, was long-established before the Aryans spread into India.

In conquering, settling and finally inter-marrying with the indigenous race of darker-skinned Dravidians who had established their own culture and traditions, the Aryans asserted themselves, so pushing the Dravidians further South into that downward-pointing triangle of India, and giving that part of the continent

7

its own particular flavour. South Indians are on the whole darker-skinned, and have differing facial structure from the Northerners – many of whom are, except for their black hair, as pale and 'Aryan' as a pure Englishman – if there is such a person, considering the mixture of our own racial stock. This goes for Pakistanis too, some of whom have blue eyes and fair hair – another indication of our linked ancestry.

The Aryans established a strong rural society based on their particularly delicate but productive breed of cattle which they had brought with them across all of Middle Asia . . . said by some authorities to be the original reason for the cult of the sacred cow. Their cattle were precious commodities in an essentially agricultural society, as the cow was also sacred to the early Egyptians. The Aryans also brought with them a marked disposition for pondering upon the awe-inspiring nature of the universe and the enormity of its comprehensiveness. These ideas were carried with them by memory in the thousands of verses of poetic philosophy which eventually were written down a thousand years later or more in books known as the Vedas.

Rig Veda
These books, especially the Rig Veda, were records of their way of life, their mystical hymns of praise, and their beliefs in the magnitude of the moving spirits or elements of the universe – fire, earth, water, wind and ether.

The Vedas
The other three Vedas came into being later. These were concerned with the sacrificial rituals around the sacred fire, the music and how it was to be composed and sung at such rites, the symbolic formula or prayer mantras invested with almost magical potency to be chanted at times of worship and in meditation (still used to this day and highlighted in recent attempts to create a cult of transcendental meditation in the West).

From this abstract content of Vedic thought history swung the pendulum over a thousand years later (around 1000 BC) to the ritualistic and formalistic side of religious worship in the Brahmin Granths.

Brahminism
From this period onwards the priestly class who later were called Brahmins, formalised the ritual and caste began to evolve and take its adhesive hold on Hinduism although it never originally existed in Vedic times. Like so many other historical developments the origins of caste have taken on mythological significance to Hindus. It is believed that the four castes originated from the body of Brahmā, the personalised form of Brahm the Godhead.

The Brahmins, the high caste, are said to have sprung from the head of Brahmā, the Kshatriyas, the soldier class from his shoulders, the Vaisyas or business and

8

trading community from his thighs, and the Sudras or lowest labouring class from the feet of Brahmā.

At this point there were no untouchables or Chandelas. Such people who were later to cast pollution upon others, because of the nature of their unsavoury labour in dealing with animal flesh and cleaning out toilets before modern hygiene revolutionised social living habits, originally grew up outside of the structure of caste because they were outcasts of society either through crime or because of punishment for social misdemeanours. Gradually – through the force of social custom (which has in every nation's society stratified social classes until recent forces of democracy began to break them down) and the later codifications of the famous Hindu law giver, Manu, of the 2nd-1st century BC – this rigidity of social division took on the aura of holy sanction.

Upanishads

This emphasis on code and ritual bred its own reactions in the forest books or Aryanakas – and the Upanishads, circa 800 BC – the most elevated questioning of the whole fundamental nature of man and his place and meaning in the cosmic world beyond his reach, which came into being as a questioning between the guru or holy teacher, and the pupil sitting at his feet.

These metaphysical concepts were at such an intellectual and spiritually refined level that naturally enough religious thought had to be brought down into terms of everyday life and concepts with which the ordinary villager could cope. There was therefore further development from pure metaphysics to a code of ethics and behaviour. So the Smritis (codes of law) and the Epics of the RAMAYANA (9th Century BC) and the MAHABHARATA (6th Century BC) evolved. It is in the latter that the 'Gem of Hindu philosophy' is to be found – the Bhagavad Gita, the Song of the Lord (Geet being the Sanskrit word for Song and Bhagavad meaning Godhead).

Bhagavad Gita

What the Bible is to Christianity, the Gita is to Hinduism. Even today in Britain in the quietude of Hindu homes, the Gita is read aloud to the children by their mothers. It is recited at ceremonies and read at the funeral pyres of cremation. Although the Mahabharata, which begins with the Gita, is in the form of an epic in the Greek manner, of a gigantic battle between warring cousins, the Pandavas and the Kauravas, the essential philosophy of Hinduism is taught by the God Krishna in the form of imagery concerning the battle within the spirit and emotion of mankind to Arjun, the princely archer of the Pāndavas whose name means 'that which is not bound'.

He speaks on the philosophy concerning a human being's duty in this world; the idea of renunciation; of selfless action dutifully undertaken without thought for the egotistical fruits of that action; of the yoga of personal self-discipline for its own inherent sake and for no other motive; of liberation beyond the confining framework of human flesh and bone into the realms of the spirit and imagination where all beauty and one-ness lies.

Culturally the Aryans brought their sense of racial superiority with them to the sub-continent as they did also to Europe which we know to our own cost in the recent Hitlerian doctrine of a pure Aryan race with the swastika as its symbol – an irony indeed as this same swastika began as a pre-Aryan emblem of great auspiciousness, again to be found in the diggings at Mohenjodaro (now in Pakistan). This emblem is used even today in Hindu decorative art and in ritual practices in temple prayer and yogic meditation.

The idea behind both the clockwise and anti-clockwise Hindu swastika is that knowledge of transcendent divinity cannot be reached through the direct line of human logic. It can only be sought after indirectly, by intuitive perception; and the crooked arms also signify 'the undetermined immensity of space' unlike the straight armed cross which expresses the expansion of space outwards but also its compression into a central point of unity.

Caste

Some Indian historians believe that the idea of caste began with the sense of colour superiority on the part of the Aryans towards the darker-skinned Dravidians with whom they integrated over the centuries in the fertile Gangetic plain. Varna (Sanskrit for 'colour' or 'features') was the original word for caste and it was the Aryan Brahmin priests who eventually took over the philosophy and ritualised it over long centuries into a static temple religion. It is only recently that the reforming, activist spirit of Hinduism has re-asserted itself through great souls like Ramakrishna, Vivekananada, Tagore and Gandhi to wrest the essential truths away from the encrusted centuries that have encased Hinduism in such rigid traditions. Caste is now outlawed by the Indian Constitution but social change cannot happen overnight.

In the world of practicalities the Aryans invented the decimal system and the mathematical rule of three, the concept of zero (shunya in Sanskrit) and the value of infinity. In fact the Arabic name for 'numerals' is 'Hindsa' – meaning 'from India'. The Aryans were also the first to chart the zodiac, to consider the rotation and gravitational influences of the planets, something now being considered by those scientists working in rocket research and the journeyings of astronauts into deep space. This led to a profound study of the science of astrology which still has a very strong influence within Indian society, especially at the time of marriage. Elaborate horoscopes are to be found in nearly every Indian family.

Astrology and Horoscopes

From time immemorial a very detailed study of the effect of the planetary system upon human behaviour, which shapes the conduct (and therefore the course) of a human being's life has been undertaken by Hindu cosmologists. Almost everybody even to this day is still much influenced by this system of study. When a Hindu baby is born a Jănămpatrika, or life horoscope, is made out by the family pandit who knows the history of generations back in the family and the influence of the planets upon their lives also. The Jănămpatrika is a scroll showing the houses of the Firmament, the zodiacal changes, the Houses of the Moon and the Sun throughout the future years. These parchments range from one foot to forty yards in length. In orthodox families they are consulted before any major events are undertaken (such as a long journey or a business transaction). Even many educated people still follow this custom which is too deeply ingrained and experienced and known to be valid, to be cast aside lightly. Especially for marriages the horoscopes of each partner are seriously studied by the family priest and often contemplated marriages are put off if the two horoscopes do not satisfactorily match. One important thing for British authorities to note is that no matter whether these are prepared by scholar or charlatan, in detail or not, the actual date and time of birth are exact and invariable and are a far more valid and authenticated document than a good many passports. Families can trace their ancestry back through generations in authentic detail in the holy centres of India where these horoscopes are kept in the safe-keeping of the family pandits or holy men.

The Aryans also evolved the comprehensive system of Ayurvedic medicine, using minerals and herbs which are now being 'discovered' by Western medical practitioners, notably in the treatment of heart and nervous disorders.

The Vedas and Hindu Ritual

Hinduism can claim no founder, no central authority like the Church, no institutional organisation, no creed. It does in fact far transcend the area of religious involvement as we know it in the West. Hinduism is a mixture of a living philosophy of the most profound kind, a temple ritual which has confused the foreigner, ancient traditions of social customs which have the strength of at least four thousand years development behind them and, recently, sweeping movements of social reform, which now find a focus in the saintly scholar Vinoba Bhave working at the humble village level and walking the face of India with nothing but a typewriter to his name.

India's religious traditions are legion but those founded on the Vedas are considered to be the highest because they have stood the storms of history and come through the tests of time, whereas other comparatively new and modern ones have vanished.

It may come as a surprise to the Westerner to be told that the world's oldest surviving faith is, in its concepts, remarkably modern. The Hymns of the Vedas emerging around 2500-2000 BC had already conceived of the truths about the universe which in the West we are only now coming to accept as scientific truths. Hindu cosmology has always worked on an immense astronomical scale the same as that now opening to us through radio-astronomy.

The early Aryan had already arrived at these concepts by another route, that of spiritual and mystical intuition. There is at least a 45 century reservoir of thought and knowledge about man and his relationship with the universe in the Hindu study of astrology, astronomy, psychology, mathematics and metaphysics.

The later Hindu Epics are full of references and stories about journeys made to the Chandra Lok (the world of the moon) and Surya Lok (the world of the sun) and many other planets. There are references to 'Amogh-shakti' – in Sanskrit an uninterceptible rocket which must hit its target – in the Mahabharata. The concept of the atom was known and the highly developed harnessing of mind and spirit and emotion to a disciplined framework of Yoga, was already 4,000 years in advance of our own psychosomatic medical discoveries. For this reason nothing is really new to a Hindu – he is an adaptive person who finds the new in the old and the ancient in the supposedly new.

The Upanishadic philosophers had also discussed creative energy in terms of modern biology – that is an evenly balanced creation of male and female principles. These abstract ideas later on appear on the mythological scene in the form of complementary deities such as Shiva and Shakti, Vishnu and Lakshmi, Rama and Sita and Krishna and Radha – which are only a few to be mentioned and worshipped every day by the Hindu peasant.

This probably accounts for the inherent equality of the gods and goddesses in the Hindu Pantheon, and also for the venerable place the Hindu woman so persistently finds in home and Indian society. In fact, because of this philosophic idea, founded upon biological principles, there has always been an acceptance of an equal balance of male and female authority which only during periods of alien invasion (such as Muslim rule from the Near East and the European Raj) became circumscribed by the need to protect women from abduction and the perils of free movement in society.

The Aryans

The early Aryans do not seem to have been idol worshippers. They reverenced nature without temples but in a polytheistic form. Nature was to them fully animated and symbolised by the God of Fire – Agni, with three forms – terrestrial as fire; atmospheric as lightning; and celestial as the sun.

Heaven and earth – 'Akāsh' and 'Dharti' – are also symbolic of vastness and brightness and their union represents the earliest Vedic conception of creation based on an indissoluble connection of these two worlds – celestial and terrestrial. Here again the basic principle of the scientific interlinking of Ether (Akāsh) and Matter (Dharti) is already significantly acknowledged by these thinkers, long before our own academic study of physics propounded the same view. Usha – Dawn, is generally described in metaphorical language, giving insight into the cosmic harmony of man and nature in optimistic and life-affirming attitudes (incidentally these Vedic names are still used as personal names for modern Indian women).

Indra, the most prominent divinity, an atmospheric God, is often identified with thunder and the wielding of the weapon – Vajra – or thunderbolt. This is the destroyer of demons, dread winds and darkness.

Surya, the Sun God, not only illuminates, but warms also, and sets life into motion with its energy. It, too, is the destroyer of darkness and ignorance, providing active life to the being. The moon, Chandra, also had a significant godly role at night but the sun is the best image of the divine used by the Aryans, Iranians and others. They worshipped all the five elements of nature: Agni – fire,

Vāyu – air, Jăl – water, Dharti – earth, and Akāsh – ether or space. Even in the myths the sun god and the moon god were not shown without female companionship – Usha, the dawn and Sandhya, the evening.

In the beginning, the Aryans did not understand the difference between body and spirit, but as the natural order of law, harmony and balance in the universe and in the forces of nature began to impinge on their intellect, these Hindu philosophers realised that independent natural forces would shatter the universe to pieces if unrelated to and uncontrolled by a single entity. The natural forces remained the object of worship but the concept of natural law behind them was given a new content and impetus. Anarchy was against the laws of being.

In their eyes the world now became an ordered Cosmos. The tendency to see order in external nature, to unify the world and place it under the control of God can result in seeing Him somewhere in or beyond space. But how can He control men? The only answer the Aryan found was that He controls from both inside and outside. Call Him Ishwara, Paramatma or the impersonal Brahm, He is the highest controlling Power, the source of light, both internal and external, and all deities therefore submit to Him. He is the Creator, the Supreme Spirit, Param Atma (the Great Soul, Atma being the personal soul).

It is sometimes said that India is a land of religions. It has indeed many branches of a single religion, i.e. Hinduism, and, therefore, many deities. Hence the charge of polytheism. The reason is that there has never been a rigidity or final sanction of the Divine Law. Man's mind and intellect has never been given to any restricted thinking in any given order, because there has been no organised or institutionalised body such as church, nor theological creed to impose an attitude of rigidity upon the Hindu mind. With the exception of Buddhism and Jainism none of the old branches of Hinduism claims revelation of spiritual truth to the exclusion of other faiths. With an exception of a few such as Islam and Christianity all religions of India are but reform movements of Hinduism, part and parcel of the Indian way of life because the content of all of them is almost the same, with similarity of method in the ways of worship for the same ultimate purpose.

What is called Hinduism in the strictest sense is based on the Vedas, also called the Shrutis (the word shruti in Sanskrit meaning 'what is heard'). The Vedas are sometimes claimed to have been heard by the sages in their forest retreats or ashrams and the truths in them said to have been revealed intuitively by 'knowing' just as the light of the sun is the direct means of our knowledge of form and colour. The Vedas are also called Shruti because their knowledge has been passed on to the pupil by the preceptor through word of mouth long before it was recorded. The Vedas are the utterances, therefore, of inspired seers known as Rishis claiming contact with the transcendental truth.

The other scriptures after the Vedas represent interpretations and codifications of that truth and are therefore called Smritis, i.e. human traditions, retained generation by generation in the form of hearing from one to the other, or recorded experience from traditions. The Hindu may also believe that his personal deity to whom he worships and whose image (often made of bronze carving) resides in his house, reveals a more explicit doctrine in some still more recent scripture.

The Hindu sees in the whole development of Hinduism the emphasis of different aspects of the Vedas, as a gradually deeper and more complete perception of the truth which was in the Vedas all the time, but which becomes clearer with the growth of man's perception over the centuries. All the six main schools of philosophy which exist within Hinduism, therefore, claim Vedic authority, a claim which later Hindus have accepted in the belief that all were complementary of the one Truth, and later movements are just continuation and expansion of an earlier faith. Even Buddhism which is sometimes considered independent of Hinduism has not rejected the authority of the Vedas.

The Trinity of Godhead

What is distinct in modern Hinduism is that sometimes Brahm or God is worshipped as Nirguna – without quality or description, and sometimes as Sagun – with quality. The latter implies worship of a personal god seen in an idol, picture or image of an object or incarnation. Although there is no watertight compartment in this case, the main personal gods are a trinity of Brahmā, Vishnu and Shiva. Brahmā is the creator; Vishnu the preserver and sustainer of the universe; and Shiva is the source of creative energy and of its ultimate destruction for the sake of further reconstruction of the good. In none of these is there idol worship – the concept behind the image is the primary concern.

Though it will be hard to find one who follows the purely Vedic traditions, there are those who at least try to do so, and are called the Arya Smajists, the society of the Aryans. Any kind of picture of God or an idol to worship is generally against their principle. They believe in God without quality or form, Brahmā as the impersonal abstract.

The Sagunists or the believers of God in a form or with quality strictly adhere to Brahmā, Vishnu, Shiva, their consorts and their progeny who gave rise to the expanding world of the Hindu Pantheon of dieties.

Brahma

Brahmā as a manifestation of the abstract idea of divinity – Brahmā is not very much worshipped, though known to every Hindu and mentioned in every religious ceremony.

Shiva

God in the form of Shiva is very popularly worshipped. Shiva has an infinite number of attributes and powers; is free from all defects and faults, Lord of the whole material and spiritual universe. He is called Bhave because he exists everywhere and at all times. He is Sarve because He destroys everything; Pasupati because He is the Lord of all physicality in the sense of animal passions; Rudra because He removes the sorrows of the world; Siva because He is free from all taints and is supremely auspicious. He is the cause of the creation, maintenance and dissolution of the world, and by His grace of the liberation of souls through the cessation of their bondage to the process of rebirth. He is enjoyer of his own infinite bliss.

In the most famous bronze image of Shiva, to be seen in the Victoria and Albert Museum in London, the conception of him is again astonishingly modern. Siva is Nata Raja, the God of Dance ringed with fire, the symbol of his aspect of Destroyer of the universe. This imagery of Godhead holds within his dancing frame the symbolism of life sparking from inert matter into the energy of motion, like particles in the gases of outer space, only to die away again in the final flames of destruction to be followed by the same cyclical process of rebirth in the sparking off of conscious energy. Philosophy and science meet within the ring of fire. He is formless when prior to creation and withdraws all his powers within himself; he is in the shape of form when he expands these powers and is about to create the world. He is not different from the creation as the snake is not different from its coils; the unity is there like the moon and its beams. He is the efficient and material cause of the world.

Through his Shakti (female energy) he creates the world. The beat of his 'Dumru' (the wasp-waisted drum still used in India by the monkey wallahs) sets the universe to dancing life, and the rhythm of his feet is the expression of the control of time and a symbol of the law of continual movement and flux in the universe into which he pours forth his energy in dancing.

On the whole the attributes of Siva are abstract and conjure up the vast principles of the universe, its forces and its relations to mankind.

Vishnu

God in the form of Vishnu is said to be the source, the transcendent God of the created worlds. In one of the famous scriptures depicting Vishnu He lies upon the waters of life which feed creation (again this could be likened to an early symbolical interpretation of the process of DNA, the nucleic acid which sustains all life) and the elementary material aspect, the first tangible emanation of the Divine, which though beyond form, yet evolves and comprehends all forms. In sculptural representation these are symbolised in the coils of the huge serpent whose dwelling is the cosmic abyss and whose name is Ananta, the Endless.

For this reason snakes are held as sacred in India and not regarded with the same evil connotations as in the West. In South India, in the groves and corners of gardens on the Malabar Coast, there is often a shrine to the Naga, or snake, and milk is placed there for the serpent's replenishment.

God as Vishnu reclines on this immeasurable body from which temporal existences spring. Ananta supports in his expanded hood both terrestrial and celestial spheres. He is the everliving cosmic ocean which is perpetually transforming its movements and its colours.

Avtar – Incarnation

The idea of Vishnu as God developed into two important forms of incarnations (chiefly Rama and Krishna) and many other avtaras as the Hindus call them. The theory of avataras or extremely holy spirits born in human form, assumes

15

divine concern for human endeavour. God is the Light in us. Our part is to open our being to this emanation. When the light in us comes to possess our being we speak of birth of God within us. The incarnation is not a special event but a continuous process of renewal of the self.

The Avtaras are born not only to put down evil but to teach mankind and to establish the codes of duty which become dissipated in the course of time and ossified by social custom.

'Dharm sansthāpanarthāye Sambhavāmi yuge yuge.' says Krishna in the Gita

'I come from age to age to re-establish codes of duties as they are needed.'

Krishna

Great souls appear for the well-being and spiritual enlightenment of creatures to tell us to remould our lives. The Divine forces are always prepared to help us provided we are prepared to call on them.

'Bhaktānam Anūkampārthanam devo vigrahāvan bhāvet,' says the Brahmā Sutra. 'Out of compassion for the devotees the Supreme assumes a human form.'

In the Hindu view such great souls have come to all mankind. Buddha, Christ and Mohammed are such ones. The Lord Krishna teaching the yoga of enlightenment in the Bhagavad Gita is their own God of redemption, the blue-skinned God of Love and devotion.

In this way there is in Hinduism what is often called 'image worship' but the way it is taken and adopted in the life of the Hindu is really symbol worship and as such is an aid to worship. The symbol is not the image. Slowly – the Hindu reasons – we get beyond the symbol to the object symbolised, until we reach the ultimate goal. We gain rewards great or small, according to our aims and objects. Image worship is a means to that realisation. When we gain our ends the means fall away. Lamps are useful so long as we live in darkness. When the sun rises they cease to be of any help.

Obviously for the ordinary generality of man, these abstract thoughts – which have no dogma nor rigid injunction to obey – have to be transformed into more concrete forms of worship.

The Temple Level

This need has brought Hindu philosophy down from its lofty heights into the world of the simple village home and the bustling market place of the temple where religion has acquired century upon century of man-made ritual, steeped in every conceivable kind of custom and superstition. Because Hinduism is so intellectually tolerant, a remarkable virtue has also become a vice, in that every manifestation of worship, no matter how tasteless or disturbing (such as animal sacrifices at Kalighat) has been tolerated.

Caste and ritual, never in original Hinduism, became prominent in Brahminical times with the rise of the priesthood to perform the many sacrifices and ceremonies as tangible signs of the inner worship of the metaphysical beliefs. These all had to be performed in the absolute correct form or else they were totally ineffective. Caste and ritual have become double-edged swords hanging over

Hindu belief. They have stabilised a society under perpetual onslaught from outside invaders (Greeks, Scythians, Parthians, Huns (Attila), Turkish Mongols and Genghis Khan who terrorised Europe as well as Asia, Moghuls, and finally British, French, Dutch and Portuguese). They have also confined and restricted society – although *within* caste there was a democracy of sorts. A Brahmin might not necessarily be born at the top of society where wealth and power reside. He might be from a very lowly Brahmin home and yet be able to mix with very powerful Brahmins at the top, so there has been more mobility vertically than in our own society where rich and poor have been clearly divided, and where the poor have suffered educationally. No matter into what circumstances a Brahmin is born, his family will have carried on the personal tradition of learning. That did not depend on wealth alone.

Certainly now the deadwood of centuries of static development is being swept away by Hindu reformers such as Ramakrishna, Vivekananda and Gandhi and Vinoba Bhave. Even Nehru would have nothing to do with this level of Hinduism and Dr Radhakrishnan, himself a high-born South Indian Brahmin philosopher-statesman, has berated the falsities of this ritualistic 'saddhu' level which has traded upon the all-believing nature of the unquestioning peasant. However, when an Indian becomes educated and lifts himself to another level, he does not necessarily jump into a sea of unbelief unlike the Western Christian rent by many intellectual doubts about the validity of truth in the Bible. Hindu philosophy creates none of this turmoil, because of its basic scientific concepts.

Puja

Gayatri Mantra

Religious worship is known as puja. It is as myriad in its forms and variety as there are individual Hindus – but of all prayers the Gayatri Mantra is as familiar and as necessary to the Hindu as the Lord's Prayer is to a Christian. It is chanted at all proper Hindu ceremonies, at birth, marriage and at formal blessings (for instance the opening of a new steel works or the inauguration of, say, the Radio Farm Forums on All India Radio) for an auspicious outcome for new undertakings.

For a child it is first properly heard at the equivalent of the Christian baptism– the mundan ceremony when the first lock of hair is cut, between the age of two and five.

This is a family ceremony in the presence of the family Pandit or priest (or the guru/teacher/priest) at a time when the child is approaching the first of the four stages of the Hindu's life on earth – that of the student or brahmacharya. In Hindu thought any child up to the age of four or five is building up images of people, values, what is right and wrong, how to behave, images which float in his consciousness but do not necessarily take on any coherence.

The taking of the sacred thread (itself symbolic, triple-threaded as it is) occurs therefore at about the age of seven when a child can correlate thoughts and events, and has some ability to understand the solemn vows undertaken as someone reborn: 'twice-born'. It is at this stage that the concept of what it is to be a dutiful and right-living Hindu first impinges on the child's mind.

Gaya means 'to sing', tri means 'three', mantra is a sung prayer or hymn. But Gayatri Mantra is embedded in further symbolism to the Hindu. It is also the Hymn of Three meanings, repeated three times with an inbuilt triple rhythm in the Sanskrit words, containing a three-fold significance in metaphysical, philosophical, and religious terms, i.e. mind, speech and body.

The thought behind this all-important Mantra is that any act initiated by a human being is limited by these three. First the vow is given in the ceremony to the Godhead – Brahmā:

'I submit to you to prepare me bodily,
Secondly to give me the power to speak right thoughts,
Thirdly to give me the power to think rightly for the sake of good.'

In Sanskrit the words are sukarm – right action
suvichār – right thought
suvachan – right speech,
implying the thought to every Hindu framed as a prayer: mansah vachan karmsah.

'I must be able to have right knowledge of the knowable
While making me a knower of the right
Because I want the knowledge for right action.'

The actual words of the Gayatri Mantra are these:
'AUM. Bhur Bhurvah Svah! Tat savitur varenyam
bhargo devasya dhimahi; dhiyo yo nah pracodayat. AUM.'

The full meaning of the Sanskrit is too subtle for the English language but an approximate translation is this:

Oh! that immanence, Glory-of-Savitri, most excellent! the effulgence of the Divine (which emanates from the solar system and the universe) let us meditate upon That!
May That (which is even incomprehensible to me it being as yet invisible) inspire me with understanding.

This Mantra should be said during the three meditations of the day – at dawn, midday and sunset. It holds the key to coming near to Godhead, and the very mouthing of its syllables is charged with a spiritual potency.

Yagyopavit

The sacred thread consisting of three strands, which again reinforces these many triple concepts a Hindu carries in his head, originated from the Vedic times and the sacred fire ceremonies or sacrifices of the horse which each King sent out to demarcate his kingdom. This was known as the Yagya or Yajna. Purification by fire is common to all mankind, even now in a medical sense, and especially in those tropical zones of the world where fire cleanses away all bacteria.

The cotton thread is placed over the boy's shoulders from left to right in the early Brahmacharya years until he becomes married and a householder when it is placed from right shoulder to left, by the guru, while sitting cross-legged in front of the sacred fire or hăwăn. This is the first yagya attended by any child of the three upper castes. The vows are taken, accepting the physical, mental and spiritual duties of being a man, and also of giving him physical, mental and spiritual fulfilment.

Daily Worship
In day-to-day life, from the time an orthodox Hindu wakes in the morning (at a very early hour – 4 to 5 am) a bath must first be taken, or a good bodily wash. (All Asians regard Westerners as very dirty people in that we are not as scrupulous about bodily cleanliness and suffer therefore much more from BO – according to their nasal reflexes). Cleansing the body is essential before prayers can be said; the act of washing in fact becomes time enough in which to meditate upon the process of prayer to come.

In such a warm climate the Hindu, if he can, goes either to a holy tank (pond) or river and immerses himself so that direct contact with natural elements is made. If a woman, she goes in, sari and all, and then skilfully unwinds into another dry sari on coming out of the water. A few personal prayers or mantras are said according to family tradition or as taught by the personal guru, while sprinkling water through the fingers in worship to the rising sun – symbol of the giver of life. In such a way humbleness of attitude is inculcated, of being part of the natural process of creation rather than as arrogant man set above nature.

After the prayer a Hindu will take up his brass lota (pitcher), fill it with water, then cast its contents away again into the river. He can equally do this at the well or in the temple and throw it over the Shiva lingam or phallic symbol of the generative processes of life creation. This black stone lingam is placed in the temple or under the spreading shade of the great peepul trees where the oxygen is most fresh in the early morning air.

The theory behind this simple ceremony is that of shrammdaan – the giving of labour in a sense of charity rather than for any expected remuneration. A Westerner seeing this may wonder why on earth the worshipper is taking up water only to throw it away again. Why so foolish? The Hindu sees this as a dedication, involving his labour without looking for any reward. Each day this becomes a constant reminder of yet another discipline to the ultimate creative process of life which will be carried sub-consciously throughout his life.

Only now can the worshipper take food – even then a tiny portion is set aside on his tala or plate before commencing his own meal, again to remind him of charity.

If he can afford it, not being of the class that has to go straight out to till the fields in the cool of the early morning before the heat reaches 115°, he goes also to the temple and is given prasād by the pandit or priest. Prasād is a word meaning kindness or beneficence and is symbolised by a sweetmeat made from milk, ghee and sugar placed in a peepul leaf plate, taken in cupped hands. Even

19

rice or a petal of a flower or a jasmin garland (never to be smelled as this would pollute it) can be given as a token of God's benevolence in the house of God. Or the priest will place a sandalwood mark – the tika – upon the forehead, or three stripes for Shiva, or a U mark for Vishnu. (The red spot worn by many Indian women, once a caste mark, is now used by single and married women universally for decorative purposes only. There are many manufactured ones also to be stuck on with nail varnish or glue.)

This kind of worship can be repeated at any time of the day – or night for that matter – as the temple is open *all* the time and one is free to enter at any time. Shoes must always be left at the door of the shrines. Each family can follow its own form of worship from long force of tradition.

There are certain times when the Gods and Goddesses are 'woken' up like human beings and take baths and are fed coconut milk, saffron and rice. These are accompanied by ringing bells and incense and the temple is flooded with classical music – and in the old days, the dedicatory temple dances of India.

Music is considered most essential in the reaching out to God in worship. It is considered in the theoretical treatise to be the preliminary basis of yoga in the concentration of mind. This has already been noticed in the West by such musicians as Yehudi Menuhin who has talked about the hypnotic state of mind, when timelessness takes over, induced by the very potent quality of Indian classical music. In fact all the creative arts have been harnessed by Hindu theorists to the worship of God, and even now in modern India most indigenous drama, dance, dance-dramas and sculpture still remain religious rather than secular in inspiration. This has implications for worship in our own schools where many Indian children are present.

In one respect Indian women are the great repositories of traditional worship. They are the keepers of the family conscience and even if the husband is not too conscientious the mother will keep all the main fasts (especially that in the late autumn for the welfare of the husband when no food is to be taken until the rising of the full moon in the last quarter of the evening), and will see that the household God is worshipped properly. She will also give alms to the wandering holy men.

Worship is always of three kinds – that which is performed daily, that which is done on particular occasions, and finally that which is undertaken for the attainment of especial regeneration or development of the soul. Hindus say:

'I take my duties put upon me by my past
and as myself in the present
and as my being, in the future through my generation'

A foreigner travelling from Cape Cormorin to the Himalayas will meet Indians almost of different nations. A Madrasi may only be able to speak to a Punjabi in English to be understood. A Hindu from Rajasthan is very different racially from a Kerala or a Bengali Indian – but they are all bound by a common background and the knowledge of their faith. Even their rituals and family customs may be radically different but without the slightest hesitation they will all understand the basic terms and important expressions of their Hindu view and way of life. This is what binds them and makes them one people.

The Upanishads and the Essential Philosophy of the Hindu Way of Life

In Sanskrit the word Upanishad approximates to the meaning in English – the nearest approach (to God). Upanish = to sit down, i.e. sitting down near a teacher to listen to his words.

Philosophically the great Upanishads wrangle with discourses of the most abstruse kind about the nature of Good and Evil, in man and the universe. It is from these questions and answers between guru and shishyu or pupil that recent Vedantic philosophy which has influenced the West, has found its inspiration. Vendanta means 'the end of the Vedas'.

One interesting thing to note is the anonymity of the Upanishadic thinkers – the rishis or learned gurus who first conceived these fundamental dialogues. This is so unlike the Greeks who put their names to their philosophical treatise perhaps because they were more aware of mortality than the Hindus.

Karma

At all levels Hinduism is concerned in a continuing dialogue between the forces of Good and Evil, right and wrong. The world is a world of action – Karma, which according to the Vedas is Duty – Dharma. A misconception held by Westerners is that Hinduism is other-worldly. The law of Karma tells us in fact that as in the physical world, in the mental and moral world also there is law, which it is the duty of every man to follow. Karma is not a theory of fatalism. It is the supreme, inescapable law of cause and effect in spiritual as well as material development. Every act has its effect on personality whether the act be thought, word or deed. This is universal law. Follow it man must, otherwise the cancer of chaos comes as it does in nature if the immutable laws are broken down and the cells explode into disorder.

The Sanskrit word for religion is also Dharma, derived from the root dhr – to hold or maintain, that which upholds the essential nature of a thing. Everything in this world has its essential nature such as burning is the essential nature of fire, inertness is the dharma of inanimate things. Similarly, a human-being has also an essential nature that upholds his existence as something distinct from the rest of creation – 'the power of becoming divine' marks out a human from all other animals.

This is Dharma through Karma – duty through action. It is meritorious Karma which sustains and supports the Universe. The creation of the world is due to Action – God had to act for it. Therefore, human action is necessary, and according to its virtue, human action can transform the nature of the universe. Past Karma has determined the present nature of the world; the present Karma can shape the future of it.

'Karmamyam Jăgăt', said the Aryan: 'World is an action'.

'Lōkōyam Karm-băndhna', says Krishna in the Gita: 'The world is bound by action.'

21

No action is ever lost. It may not produce an immediate effect, and it remains in latent form until proper occasion for fructification comes. It becomes a potential energy. This is a highly activistic faith, and its doctrine is not merely fatalism. Our acts determine our character which in turn determine our acts. This emphasises the importance of conduct. It lays a heavy responsibility on each individual Hindu to strive towards his own salvation from his own inner 'call' towards good, and yearning for it, rather than because of outward admonishments arising from an external dogma, theology or commandment saying THOU SHALT or THOU SHALT NOT.

The law of Karma is simply the organic nature of life where each successive phase grows inevitably from what has gone before and where humanity, and therefore each individual as part of a gigantic whole, is subject to universal laws which hold everything in right balance. It intensifies our sense of the tremendous importance of every decision we make for the right or the wrong. This has not been made clear enough to the Western world. It has in fact nothing in common with pre-destination as is commonly supposed. It is the inescapable logic of the universe and pre-supposes the necessity of personal discipline, an inner authority, which impels us to obey the order of things.

The Logic of Law and Authority

It rather affirms that by doing what is in our power we can dispose the mind to the love of the Eternal and so attain salvation. This has been the central core of every branch of the Hindu religion, and is as relevant today in the present world situation as it was long ago.

Even the illiterate peasant shows an inate awareness of this philosophy despite lack of formal knowledge. Illiteracy does not necessarily preclude wisdom. He trudges along hundreds of miles by bullock cart or on foot to the great Kumbh melas or festivals where he will bathe in the sacred waters at the time of certain planetary conjunctions or eclipses of the sun or moon. This may be due to superstition and ritual but he also recognises the same concepts as the more intellectual Hindu. This is always a constant surprise to anyone coming to India for the first time – no matter how lacking in formal education, there resides in the ordinary villager an astonishing wisdom and intuitive knowledge of the basic philosophical concepts behind the poetic truths of the Epics, and the Upanishads.

Dharma

The concept of Dharma is as important and popular among Indians as that of Karma. In Sanskrit the word has many overtones, meaning equally DUTY, QUALITY, ENTITY, NATURE, RIGHT CONDUCT, MERIT, RELIGION, LAW, JUSTICE and even REALITY. For a long period it has been considered both as meaning 'right' and 'good'; it was accepted that whatever was good and right was Dharma.

Maya and Moksha

For all schools of Indian religion and philosophy man is a wayfarer –

Margayan – from the outward world to inward reality – i.e. the ultimate truth. During this journeying, man yearns for liberation – Mukti or Moksha– a liberation from the prisonhouse of human ignorance which makes an illusion – Maya – of our existence. The *real* reality is *not* the tangible world we see around us in material terms but the illusive inner core of our beings (closer to the concept of spirit in the Christian sense). God is within each one of us in the very fact that we exist. The scientific process of creativity is God. Divinity is us. The Sanskrit saying is: TAT TWAM ASI – THOU ART THAT.

The philosophical books are full of discourses on individual atma or soul in relation to the measureless Reality or great Soul – Param Atma, otherwise called Perfection or the Impersonal Absolute, of which all of us are but minute parts, individual molecules enmeshed in an immense living whole.

Karma in accordance with Dharma is a means through which liberation or Mukti is achieved. Dharma determines the course of Karma. Right knowledge therefore is necessary to tear away the curtains of illusion known as Maya.

Maya

Maya is human ignorance, or knowledge without the rightful corollary of wisdom (an entirely different thing). Such knowledge leads to false ideas through un-controlled passions. For this, the importance of the Guru – the competent guide and teacher – has been considered so important by all branches of faith and learning that sometimes the Guru is placed as high as Godhead itself.

The Guru

It is said in Sanskrit:

Guru Brahma, Guru Vishnu, Guru Devo Maheshvaraha
Guru Sakshat, Param-Brahma, Tasmai Shree Guru-ve namam'.

'I bow down therefore in homage to my Guru (preceptor) who not only represents the Trimurti (the three images of the Trinity, Brahma, Vishnu, and Shiva) but also the whole Universe (Param-Brahma) incarnate'.

This is the reason for due reverence still being given to the teacher in India. The Guru will choose the way he finds suitable and easy for the disciple or shishyu according to the intellectual and spiritual state of the devotee.

The goal is the same – liberation of the individual soul from the imprisoning sense of Maya, and the merging of that soul into the Great spirit, Param Atma, the Brahm. This is the highest duty of man, to lift the human soul to that standard where it is absorbed into the real life where union with Godhead is achieved. This has led the Hindu to a very alive and constant concern with investigating the true nature of reality in his personal thinking and with a detached sense of illusion where the world around him is concerned.

Faith is a very personal, individual discipline for the Hindu and cannot be dogmatised over by religious bodies. Each person's salvation is his own concern and a matter for his own searching, will power and devotion. This may explain why, in general, the Indian accepts more passively the upheavals of life rather than turning to the rebellious attitudes characteristic of the West. The restless ferment, change for change's sake, is not the concern of the Hindu. The search is constantly into personality, into the inner reality. It may also account for his adaptability to new conditions and environments as he is only beholden to his own moral conscience. An Indian enjoys perhaps the widest ranging intellectual liberty of any religious worshipper. He is on his own with God to come to terms with the ultimate values of life. Each Indian is his own Socrates, Plato, St Augustine and Bertrand Russell rolled into one!

The highest kind of education therefore, through the Guru, is that which enables the individual to evolve himself to deeper awareness, a process of evolution from material existence to that of the spirit corresponding to the evolutionary development in biological terms, improving on the creative forms of life through long aeons of experiment and survival of the best adjusted forms of that life.

Thus at the level of spirit also, man slowly moves forward as he realises the need to improve to bring the atma to the level of the Great Atma, the level of Deity. This is his deep, just and meritful duty to achieve.

Moksha or Mukti

The realisation of this urge to improve upon what is, to search out perfection in one's self, is the road towards Salvation – Moksha – a release from the process of death and rebirth which Karma demands until the final union with the Absolute Perfection. Towards this end, all Hindu processes of worship are directed, either through personal daily worship, known as puja, in which prayers are said to a family deity and flowers, coconut milk, ghee, saffron and sweets are offered up. Or the worship can be undertaken in the personal hardship of long pilgrimages on foot, as is still very common in India both by the under-privileged villager and the most intellectually progressive modern city dweller; or through the directing of mind in concentrated meditation, through the remarkable control of body and mind in the processes of Yoga.

The Hindu believes that he will be rewarded for good deeds through the growth of reincarnation, and at the lowest level within the temple even, ritual rightly and specifically performed, will be meritorious and his process of salvation will be quickened. This is why the temple level of Hinduism has remained so entrenched and important. Bad deeds, however, will retard this process. One bad act will put him in the yoke of a thousand more births and rebirths, an infinitely wearying process, and thus delay the union of his atma with God.

Besides, says the Hindu, you cannot escape the effect of the cause. You must be rewarded for the good deed and punished for the bad Karma, the evil side of your active life, mental, physical or whatever you may call it. It is because of the ultimate logic of this system of thought, and the justice of it, that the doctrine of reincarnation has such a strong hold on the Hindu mind. There is no escape from the evil and the punishment due for it in this life or the next life beyond this one.

24

There is always certainty of the reward for good deeds and a good heart now and hereafter. This is why Hindu literature is full of hope without the slightest sense of tragedy until foreign influences through European literature, with its pessimistic strain, appeared in India and began to influence Indian thought (although only indirectly). The sense of inescapable sin born as original sin within the West, so tarnishing us from birth, even in sexual conception, and giving fraility to life is wholly foreign to the Hindu view of life. This is why the creative processes of life and anything to do with sex are not regarded with any of the overtones of original sin. This is an abhorrent idea to the Hindu and it is only since the British Raj and the advent of Christian missionaries that an ambiguous attitude to sex has arisen, confused by a wholly foreign Victorian prudery. In fact in early Hindu society, a man's life span was divided into four stages so that mental, physical and spiritual were in an entirely harmonious balance. The first stage was that of the chela, or brahmachārya student, devoted to study; the second that of the grihasthya or householder who was to enjoy family life, sex and wealth; the third stage was the retirement slowly from social life to that of the forest, vānaprasthya – and finally to the hermit life of the sannyāsi.

Indians can accept family planning with complete intellectual and moral freedom. Their only need in a predominantly rural society of at least 600,000 villages is to produce sons to help on the land and to take care of the family when parents are aged.

According to this doctrine of reincarnation it takes thousands of rebirths (the layman knows this as 'chorassi lakh', 84 lakhs, a lakh being the equivalent of 10,000) to enable the individual ego, atman or soul to burn away the dross of evil, and gradually reach that higher state of awareness in future lives until the final submerging with the Brahm is attained.

'Why don't you believe in the evolution of the soul in the same way that you believe in the evolution, in a biological sense, of material life?' is what the Hindu asks.

One life is too short to perfect the individual Atma. After all, how many aeons in the process of evolution it has taken to perfect man biologically from the ape! Man still seems lacking in too much in the search for spiritual perfection. Yet the Hindu reasons that despite our wayward natures the knowledge is unconsciously there that we must inevitably move towards goodness once we know how to harness these subconscious urges as, slowly, our ignorance, in terms of the subtle body of spirit, is stripped away like the layers of an onion. When the price for wrong acts has been duly paid and we have had time enough to till the ground and to nourish it, sowing the seeds in many lives, the time matures for the harvest to be reaped in its own patiently awaited time. It is this reason that gives the Hindu mind its tranquility of spirit in a slow, unhurried way which many Westerners misunderstand as a lack of urgency. Life to the Indian, however, has no clearly defined horizon at its far edge; it has stretched too far back, and stretches far away into the future. Immortality is life, in the past, here and now, and in the future. Sometimes at funerals in India the draped body is taken to its cremation accompanied by a band of male relatives singing with rejoicing at a long life lived rightfully. Death is not always an occasion for weeping.

The place of the Epic Poems, Ramayana and Mahabharata

The ordinary Hindu does not follow all this abstract philosophy intellectually but almost by instinct.

Indian children have heard all the philosophy in the mythological tales passed on from their parents, forefathers and the family priests. Many have the Gita read to them at night and sit silently watching their mothers performing simple worship in the home done in true devotion every morning of their lives. Sometimes on a mantleshelf over an English fireplace the picture of Shiva or Krishna, or a cheap calendar drawing in garish colours, will serve as the shrine, surrounded by flowers and incense. Prayers will be said quietly and the hands placed together in 'namesteh' greeting, morning and night. Puja is done discreetly but it is nevertheless done – and almost universally in Hindu homes.

Sometimes in the villages and suburbs of the towns there are the wandering holy men and minstrels (like mediaeval troubadors) singing the same stories, accompanied by colourful stringed instruments and drums. The philosophical ideas which would seem to be above the heads of simple people are not complicated ones to the Indian, as they pervade the very atmosphere and are alive in day-to-day life.

Above all Hindu scriptures, the two great Epics have exercised the most influence upon the people of India, and in later centuries from the 7th century onwards, throughout the lands of S.E. Asia also – Thailand, Cambodia, Indonesia and Bali especially.

It is their mixture of dramatic myth, historical legend, vividly recounted personalised stories of the Gods, that enabled the high-flown philosophy to be brought down to the level of the man in the street. The metaphysics are there but in parable or allegorical form woven around Krishna in the Mahabharata as an incarnation of Vishnu, the God of the Trinity, and around Rama, again another avtar of Vishnu, in the Ramayana.

The nearest analogy in Western terms would be if the Iliad and Odyssey of Greece were liberally combined with the main sections of the Christian New Testament, and schools of modern philosophy into a non-academic way of life.

Ramayana

The Ramayana is very different from the martial Epic of its successor. Here the values of bravery, truthfulness and especially loyalty are stressed in a somewhat didactic and practical manner.

But the atmosphere of the Ramayana is tinged with a lyricism and an idealism which makes every character represent a type towards which each Hindu should attempt to attain. It tells the story of Rama, Prince of Ayodhya, a northern kingdom in Uttar Pradesh, who is at the same time the ideal husband of Sita; the ideal brother of Lakshmana; the ideal son of the King of Ayodhya; the ideal warrior; the ideal friend; and the ideal devotee. In Indian schools, even Christian convent schools, Indian children of all faiths are taught to revere Rama as the essence of what a man should try to be, and Sita as the ideal of womanhood – chaste, modest and all-obedient to her husband. Even the birds, animals and plant life seem to exude a poetic state of optimistic joy and reverence, and are 'alive' to the dharma, the eternal order of right living.

The unjust exile of Rama, the capture of Sita by the demon-king Ravana (regarded by some Indians as more a mixture of a fallen angel rather than an outrightly wicked villain), the rescue of Sita by an army of monkeys headed by the inventive Hanuman, the Monkey God (the reason for the sacred nature of India's vast monkey population) have all inspired countless subsidiary tales and dramas and dance poems like the Mahabharata has also done.

At a more subtle level of influence, the Ramayana has become a holy book to the Hindu. Rama, because of the nature of his incarnation, is also a God to whom Hindus bow down in reverence and upon whom they call when the bodies are taken down to the burning ghats.

'Rām, Rām, naam satya hai' is the cry.
'The name of Rama is truth'.

As symbol of the divine forces of goodness, the whole story of his eventual reunion with Sita spells out the conflict between good and evil and the eventual overcoming of the latter. This is enacted out year by year over the centuries in the village Kātha or dramas of the Ramalila, in the colourful and dramatic Hindu festival of Dussehra which takes place some time in September/October, and in the folk songs of the itinerant musicians and holy men. It is not known by formal scripture lesson but by the immediacy of a living culture which is very much 'in the air' of India.

Mahabharata

The historical development and enlargement of the Mahabharata (the longest single poem in the world, consisting of 200,000 verses seven times the length of the two Greek epics combined) took well over a thousand years to achieve its present form – from about 900 BC when a historical battle was fought at Kurukshetra in the Punjab, up to about AD 500 when it was finally written down.

The enduring story of the battle between cousins, the Pandavas and the Kauravas; the romantic story of Damayanti, the beautiful princess and Nala, her Prince Charming; the lyrical love story of Shakuntalla (as famous in India as Hamlet is in Britain) – these have all served as the root themes for infinite variations in Indian literature right up to the present age. They have also influenced and been depicted in sculptural form upon the temple walls, in the exquisite miniature paintings by *Muslim* artists in the Moghul period, and in the evocative poetry both of pure literature and of love songs in classical dance forms of Bharata Natyam and the stylised mime-dance of Kathakali.

Dussehra

This autumn festival which culminates in the beautiful feast of Diwali – or Deepavali, the Festival of Lights – takes ten days to celebrate. During this time the whole of the Ramayan is acted out by strolling players in the true Shakespearean tradition and the final drama reaches the full heights of excitement upon the open spaces or maidans of North Indian cities.

As the flaming arrow from Rama's bow (an ordinary human actor) speeds into the gigantic papier mâche figures (incidentally made by Muslim craftsmen) of the demon King, Ravana and his brother and son, these burst into flames amid a great roar from the thousands of people gathered around, no matter whether they are Muslims, Christian, Sikh, Parsee, Jain or Buddhist. The triumph of good over evil, the yearning for this to be so, is universal.

These colossal Epics, encyclopaedias of tradition and legend, carry a storehouse of continually replenished Indian thought, inspiration and social commentary, which unlike Greek philosophy has not been relegated to an intellectual exercise in the classroom or to the academicians. Because these epics have seeped into the whole of Indian life they are permanently alive even in the most modern and seemingly sophisticated Indians of the twentieth century.

Yoga

The Sanskrit word Yog has the same connotations as the English word Yoke – meaning togetherness, or binding together.

In the Western mind yoga is associated with body-twisting gymnastic exercises. The Hindu concept is very different indeed, seeing these specific, scientifically worked out postures as only a means to a much more comprehensive end. Through an efficiently run bodily system and properly concentrated breathing the mind can be so directed that body is finally forgotten.

To the Hindu philosophers the theory that 'mind is matter' was not something to talk about theoretically in philosophical tomes, but a concept upon which to act. Mind is not physical matter but 'subtle' matter – we become what we think. This is why prayer and meditation still have such an emphatic hold even upon seemingly agnostic modern Indians. There can be no atheists in the Hindu view. No matter how much we deny God, we *are* God by the very nature of our creation.

The discipline therefore of Yoga is not concerned with the mechanics (the āssnas or postures) but with the abstract idea of freeing ones self from all earth-binding desires through control of the bodily system to such an extent that attainment 'with the impersonal infinite from which all things arise' is reached.

The Eight Stages of Yoga

To achieve this end, being in the world but not of the world, eight progressively difficult stages of yoga evolved. These are:
1. the curbing of instincts
2. disciplinary preparations
3. postures (āssnas)

4. breathing control (prānayām)
5. withdrawal of senses and movement
6. fixation of thought
7. meditation (dhyāna)
8. samādhi – the final goal; with fixation of the psyche upon the infinite.

According to Krishna in the Gita the purpose of Yoga is to attain 'unwavering firmness by which one restrains the activity of the mind' – mānah; of the life-breath – prāna; and of the sense organs; the firmness which is pure, so essential to direct the mind, the body to the inner sources of energy or soul in a mystical and divine sense.'

The resources are there within each human being but for the asking – and with right knowledge. But again a guru is necessary because the evolution of soul is an extremely delicate matter and the processes of yoga are so demanding as to be extremely dangerous to the uninitiated.

The final aim of yoga is toward liberation from the claims of self – that is forgetfulness of self.

Mukti or Moksha has been mentioned before but to Indians whether they go to the temple to worship in a more ritual way in the simplicity of faith, or to those who reach up to the mystical philosophy, the concern about the purpose of life is both more clearly defined and yet more complex than meets the eye.

The purpose of life

Everything that lives aims at the specific perfection of its own nature. The sub-human species work according to a pre-determined pattern but man due to his creative will has to achieve fulfilment by his effort and will. Man is not completely a victim of circumstances. He can say 'NO' to life and he can reject one kind of satisfaction for that of a higher kind. He can impose discipline on his nature and check the drive of desire. He can create a new nature in which the different elements of his being are harmonised. To the Hindu there is a strain in human life which impels us to introduce peace and order into the swarm of impulses, emotions and notions which are basically incongruous to the harmony of our own souls. To bring harmony in this field is a job which will take more than a lifetime. But humanity has an ache for perfection and wholeness and an anguish for beatitude. Man's quest for perfection consists in organising things of body, mind and soul into a unity to attain the kingdom of heaven. So long as our natures are not integrated, our actions are confused and contradictory. In an integrated man thought, speech and action are of one piece. Yoga aims at integration of all the parts of a human being into a perfected whole.

Unity in Diversity

Unity in diversity is such a perennial theme in India it has now become a political platitude.

Since each person is unique his way to fulfilment is unique, and must be his own. But there is so much in common between human beings that certain ways to man's realisation of perfection can be differentiated. In the Hindu view they are the

1. KARMA MARGA – the way of action
2. BHAKTI MARGA – the way of devotion
3. DHYAN MARGA – the way of meditation

All the ways lead to Gyana, wisdom or enlightenment. And Yoga includes the different aspects of work – Action, Devotion and Knowledge.

The principle of **Karma Marga** has already been discussed independently.

Bhakti Marga or the way of devotion, (bhakti meaning intense loving devotion) has been accepted generally by every Hindu. It asserts that it is only through loving devotion that one can attain the unattainable. The way of devotion presupposes the recognition of a personal God (more in the sense of a loving God who cares for His children) who is omniscient, omnipresent, omnipotent, who confers His grace on the devotee, however lowly he may be, when he surrenders himself unreservedly to Him. The devotee finds Supreme pleasure in God. Love of man and woman is commonly used to illustrate love of man for God. When the lovers are together they are afraid of being separated, when they are not together they have a painful desire for union, as is seen in the yearning desire of Radha for Krishna in his aspect as the playful Cupid, the blue-skinned God with his flute playing so effectively upon the heartstrings of the milkmaids who encircle him – this is a symbolism for the whole of humanity.

The followers of this way believe that liberation or realisation or perfection is possible only through devotion of the devotee's soul which itself is the part of the Great Soul – Param Atma. Even reason and intellect may become tangled through Maya (the illusion of objects around us) whereas devotion moves on undeterred. Devotion means complete and exclusive absorption in God and is indifferent to things opposed to Him. It is a fruit in itself. God loves the meek, and devotion implies obedience to the will of the Supreme in all man's activities. Choosing this path, the Hindu is free to choose his own personal God, male or female: to worship a representative image of the Deva which is usually kept in a niche and decorated with flowers and saffron in the privacy of the home.

Hindu Pantheon of Deities

Out of this has arisen the huge Hindu pantheon of Gods and Goddesses, representing every kind of human yearning, even to the darkest side of man's nature in the blood lust cult of the dark Goddess of Destruction of Bengal – Kali. This multitude of aspirations has given rise to the idea that Hindus are polytheistic by nature but scratch the surface of a Hindu and underneath he will be seen to resolve the multitude into a wholeness or unity – the one God. Singularity comes from the multifarious.

Dhyan Marga or the Way of Meditation

The way of meditation is itself a part of the Yoga system. There is a broad stream of spiritual knowledge in us. It requires us to grow to a higher level of being by an inner quickening and growth in our nature. The all-pervading Self abides in every heart. By discipline of mind, we should strive to apprehend the Real. Our vision becomes obscure if it is dimmed by vice and weakness. The Mahabharata says: 'The Supreme is visible only to those who have overcome anger and mastered their senses.'

In moments of meditation we become self aware. With this yogic ability to control our senses we do not lose the feel of the eternal in the distractions of life; rather we acquire a trust that sustains us in the most terrible catastrophies. We gain a firm loyalty to truth in the midst of passions and lure. This method of yoga system gives us processes by which our consciousness grows into the life of the divine by the control of thinking mind.

Conclusion

A Hindu is therefore neither under an obedience to a divine revelation in historic time, nor is he bound to a form of worship in accordance with the contents of that revelation. It has been said that 'the essential core of Hinduism is free from all dogmatic affirmations of who God is – TRUTH in fact transcends all verbal definitions thought up by man.'

Dr Rajagopalachari, India's nonagenarian statesman/philosopher has written: 'Indian philosophy lays the greatest stress on an attitude not merely of passive tolerance but active respect for different forms of worship. It is the exact opposite of the doctrine of exclusive truth on which Christianity and Islam sincerely and seriously insist.'

Each Hindu has in the final analysis to find his own pathway to that end; each image of a God or Goddess is there to help the devotee in his own personal vision of the God. But at the end there are no divisions, no differences, no separate entities. Each is part of the one. In the words of a Christian mystic, John Donne, of the 17th Century:

> 'No man is an Iland, intire of itselfe;
> every man is a peece of the Continent,
> a part of the maine.'

This is the essence of Hinduism.

Bibliography

The Hindu View of Life, Dr Sarvapalli Radhakrishnan; Publisher: George Allen & Unwin, London.
The Brahma Sutra – Text and Explanation, Translated and with an introduction by Dr S. Radhakrishnan; Publisher: George Allen & Unwin, London.
Bhagavad Gita – Sanskrit and English Version, translated by Dr S. Radhakrishnan; Publisher: George Allen & Unwin, London.
Bhagavad Gita – Sanskrit and English Version, Annie Besant, G. A. Natesan, Madras.

Hinduism, The World's Oldest Faith, Professor K. M. Sen; Pelican Book, 3/6d,
Ramayana, C. Rajagopalachari; Publisher: Bharatiya Vidya Bhavan, Chaupatty, Bombay, 1957.
Mahabharata, C. Rajagopalachari; *Hindustan Times*, New Delhi.
The Indian Heritage, by Professor Humayun Kabir; Asia Publishing House, London, 1946.
Hindu Society at Crossroads, K. M. Panikkar; Asia Publishing House, London.
The Holy Lake of the Acts of Rama, Tulasi Das; translated by W. D. P. Hill; Oxford University Press, 1952.
Eastern Religious and Western Thought, Dr S. Radhakrishnan; Clarendon Press, Oxford.
The World's Great Religions, Special Edition. *Life Magazine;* Collins, London and Glasgow.
Sources of Indian Tradition – 2 volumes, Introduction to Oriental Civilisations, editor Wm. Theodore de Bary; Columbia University Press, New York & London.

ISLAM

by

Mohammed Iqbal

'There is no God but Allah . . . and Muhammed is His Prophet'

Of all the world's universal religions Islam is the last in historical development, coming into existence in the 7th Century after Christ's birth. For those who profess to be Muslim it is the most clearly defined. It is at the same time the most clearcut religion to follow – hence its widespread appeal to people of all nations.

The Arabic word ISLAM literally means 'Submission to the Will of God', and MUSLIM means 'the one who submits'. Dr Ali Khan, Assistant Editor of the *Islamic Review*, has enlarged upon this, pointing out that it is not only submission. Islam actually means a system which 'enables a Muslim to get into a state of peace and the state free from vice and defect; also it enables him to cause all kinds of peace to others. The message of Islam reminds men of endless possibilities and his boundless capabilities, and places in front of him some fundamental truths of science in order to open up a way for his progress and understanding. For instance it tells him that he can go to other planets (Quran 55:34) and that there are atmospheres and gases on other planets (Quran 6:12) that the planets float in their orbits (Quran 36:38:40).'

Islam bows down in worship to a single all-powerful God, Allah, who manifested himself through the Archangel Gabriel to one Prophet, Muhammed, who was according to tradition, born in Mecca in AD 570. This revelation which was miraculously sustained over a period of years, was taken down by Muhammed's followers on 'scraps of parchment and leather, camels' shoulder-blades and ribs, pieces of board and the hearts of men', and collected into 114 chapters called suras, which have been compiled into the Muslim Holy Book.

This outpouring of divine inspiration through the medium of the great Prophet is called the Quran (meaning a reading). It is the repository of all truth about life, all that a Muslim must do as a human being in this world, how he must order his family life, his finances and what he passes on as inheritance, his eating habits, his moral codes. These are very strictly defined and as the Quran is accepted as the last and final revelation of Allah, there is no further commentary to be made on the ordering of human life. This intensity, and the concentrated worship it has inspired, has created a self-contained culture and a self-sustaining civilisation stronger than in any other faith – its goal is human success in this life as well as in the next.

Although there is a common ancestry to both Christianity and Islam, there are fundamental differences in the concept of Godhead – to a Muslim Allah is indivisible and there is no sense of the Trinity of the Christian God. There are, however, many meeting points between Islam and Christianity. The Quran is the actual Word of the indivisible God in much the same way as those words of Christ spoken directly to his disciples in the New Testament. The difference lies in the fact that the former is the final and unchanged word, whereas the Bible has undergone change and critical analysis. The Quran is the collection of revelations made to Muhammed through the Archangel Gabriel. In this sense Muhammed can be said to be the interpreter of Allah's message. Direct confrontation with God came in later Muslim development in the magnificent singing poetry of the Sufi mystics.

In Persia in the 9th Century ascetics known as Sufis (wool wearers – Suf meaning wool), retired from the world into monasteries or wandered the roads creating a new tradition of mystic poetry, which sang with intense out-pouring and joyousness of mystical union with God. This ecstatic state of religious faith came into existence when Muslim culture responded to the Greco-Roman Byzantine and Persian heritage and the influence of other world religions.

The ascetics of those days and the present time are, however, all required to abide by and practice the teachings of the Quran and Muhammed's sayings if they claim to be Muslims. There are only a small number of ultra-spiritualists among the followers of Islam. To lead a successful life requires striking a balance between extremities. Perhaps it will not be out of place to mention here the novel behaviour of the ascetics. An act done by a Muslim mystic might appear to be wrong according to the dictates of the holy Quran and Hadith but in fact may be in conformity with it in the mystic codes.

One instance is the case of Al-Hallaj who rose to such a stage of Sufism that he broke the traditional barriers and declared himself God, which the Islamic jurists of that day challenged there and then. For this breach he was persecuted and finally executed in Baghdad in AD 922.

Islam has in fact *never* encouraged its followers to resign the worldly life in order to engage in such exclusively individual meditative pursuits. Such mystical union with the Creator is regarded as coming *last of all* in a man's religious development which begins essentially with orthodox traditional practice of the basic tenets of Islam.

Muhammed's ascension into Heaven through piety and love for mankind has, of course, been the virtuous inspiration for Sufi belief. But this is only one of many aspects of his life. A Muslim who follows Muhammed in all the many facets of his life can surely aspire to be distinguished amongst mankind and near to the Creator.

The following Prayer of Unity, a sura (injunction) from the revelations of Muhammed, is what the average Muslim should keep most in mind, and exemplifies the essential truth of the Muslim view of the definition of the Creator.

'In the name of Allah, the Beneficent, the Merciful!
Say: He is Allah, the One!
Allah, the eternally Besought of all!
He begetteth not, nor was begotten.
And there is none comparable unto Him'.

the Prayer of Unity from the Quran.

The Historical Background

Much of the teaching of the Old Testament and the general understanding of the creation of mankind from Adam and Eve, has been handed down to the followers of Islam. A Muslim firmly believes that these are the outcome of religious revelations and injunctions communicated to the Prophets from time to time. The Holy Sermons of Muhammed clearly accept the Scrolls of Moses, the Psalms of David and the Gospel of Jesus as books sent by God to the prophets in a set chronological order. One great festival of the Islamic year, Eid-ul-Adha, sometimes spelled Zuha in English, in fact is done in remembrance of Abraham's near sacrifice of Ishmael, (Christians believe it was Isaac) his son. Other spiritual books or prophets, other than those specifically mentioned in the Quran, are not countenanced.

From the Muslim point of view the founders of Hinduism and Buddhism and the authors of the Hindu Vedas and the Buddhist Canon can neither be accepted nor rejected categorically as Prophets in the sense that Christ is accepted along with Moses, Elija and Abraham as Prophet of the One Indivisible God.

Moreover, the authenticity of the Divine Books of the Old Testament referred to in the Old Testament constituted the beginnings of Islam. These books, other than the Quran, have undergone many changes, having been handed down under the prevailing circumstances of oral traditions during long historical times, and they are far from their original forms. But the striking resemblance of certain narrations in these books, however, are strong enough points to prove their divine source.

The story of Abraham's sacrifice, for instance, in both the Old Testament and the Quran proves its authenticity and trustworthiness. Some of the four-thousand-year-old beliefs, teachings and practices of Judaism are again akin to those of Muslims and hence the authenticity of their basis. Circumcision and ritual slaughter of animals for human consumption are common to both Jew and Muslim.

The Quran is complete to a Muslim as the revelation of God, and one who knows the general methods of its compilation and the presentation of its teachings will begin to understand that there are no deletions or additions. The Quran, originally in Arabic (the subtlety of which can never be given proper justice by the more concise English translations) is complete in all respects and provides systematic guidelines of a fundamental nature to all kinds of people, no matter their nationality, at all times in history.

The Spread of Islam

Like Christianity, Islam is a prosletysing faith. So great was the revelation in meaning to Muhammed the Prophet that he undertook the ordinance to spread its word and the teachings of Allah's inspiration to the pagan tribes of Saudi Arabia where he was born.

Alongside the Quran, there grew up a collection of Muhammed's sayings (explanations of the revelations of Allah, and temporal matters – about 10,000 reports altogether) which have supplemented the Quran to a great degree.

These are known as the Hadith (pronounced Hadeez). In any problematical situation or personal moral crisis reference can be made not only to the Quran but to this whole tradition of juridicial interpretation.

These have been the basis for the strong impetus to take the message of Allah all over the globe. In the initial stages Islam was preached among (*a*) heathens, (*b*) Jews and (*c*) Christians. The pagan tribes in Mecca, Saudi Arabia, were idol worshippers and polytheists. They accepted in multitudes the message of the Great Prophet in bettering the order of society which prevailed at the time. One has to remember the context in which Islam emerged amid the feuding tribes of Arabia, in a backward uneducated desert society where there was much ignorance and apathy towards any spiritual life.

'Virility', which helped each Arab to inculcate in himself the qualities to defend himself and his tribe, was prevalent all over the society of old Arabia. Justice was indeed rough justice, hardly tempered with mercy, a case of 'an eye for an eye, a tooth for a tooth'.

The Quran arrived with the impact of a thunderbolt, giving the Arabs a code to 'do good and forbid evil'. For the first time forgiveness or pardoning is recommended as a counter-balance for their harsh code of summary justice. Muhammed taught that man is created in the image of God who has various and manifold images. This is where the uniqueness of human character both in shape and mind is apparent, and the quality of the relationship of each human individual with God is manifested. This has influenced the attitude of Muslims towards the government and the role of the State.

The Building-up of an Islamic Society

The head of an Islamic State, it is ordained according to the ideal, must be the humblest and the most knowledgeable of all the subjects and is regarded as the servant of the people, enjoying the same equal rights as they do – but no more according to positions of status. Islam rejects the age-old conception of special privileges for the Head of State. As a matter of fact the early Khalifahs (the Caliphs) of Muhammed – The Apostle of God – who ruled the vast lands consisting of existing Saudi Arabia and areas from the countries around her left historic and practicable traditions for the Muslim Kings devout to the cause of Islam in times to come.

Abu-Bakr, the first Caliph, was known as the man of two pins, because he always wore a single garment which he used to pin together. Umar-b-Alkhitab, the second Caliph, who ruled the world in its entirety had the treasures of Chosroes and Caesar at his disposal but lived on bread and olive oil and wore clothes with innumerable patches. Uthman, the third Caliph, used to carry faggots of firewood on his shoulders and once, when he was asked the reason he did so, simply said, 'I wanted to know if my soul would refuse'.

When Ali succeeded, he maintained the ascetic traditions of his predecessors and is said to have bought a shirt for five darhams (coinage system) and finding the sleeves too long caught hold of a cobbler's knife and cut off the sleeves level with the tips of his fingers. This served to set an example of discipline and self-abnegation for those in positions of authority, especially in the beginnings of Muslim society when so much that had existed before Muhammed was based on total privilege.

The Idea of Equality

A remarkable feature of Islamic ideology is the principle of 'balance'. Islam has laid down the general rule of adopting the middle path in man's outlook as well as in his actions. To a Muslim, other religions seem to appear one-sided – sacrificing either this world or the next. Islam tries to strike a happy balance between the demands of this world and the requirements of the next. Fundamentally Islam is concerned with a spiritual democracy, so much so that there has never been a priestly hierarchy or a dynasty of religious leaders who might act as intermedaries between man and God. The Imam is not the equivalent of the Christian priest. In each mosque he is responsible only to himself and not to a bishop, or to a body of the Church. Even in Islamic society, the ideal is a classless social order in which the only criterion for preference and superiority is that of character.

Muslim political democracy is defined as 'the Government of God for the people by the people'. The ruler is required to carry out the commands of the Holy Quran and Hadith, and the ability to do so is the only reason for placing the ruler above others. When Islam emphasises the sovereignty of God it means that no human being has the right to rule over other human beings.

Through Muhammed, pagan society was therefore totally transformed. Morality and piety were merged into each other, and the later influence of Sufism refined and selectively added to its credit by taking on itself the intense personal mystic love of God as the basic vehicle of all actions done for God's sake.

The moral degeneration and corruption in all aspects of life among the Arab pagans in the 6th-7th centuries AD required a mentor and a prophet of excellent example and of a resolute character. The dire situation, morally and materially, demanded the exemplary behaviour of converts at the beginning and force was of course used when the first followers of Muhammed were attacked by the outraged merchants, who thrived on the pilgrim trade to Mecca where pagan believers worshipped at the shrine of the Kaaba (a cube). This rectangular structure contained certain idols and a black meteorite which had fallen there from the heavens.

Persecution of the newly formed Muslim groups in Mecca, in fact caused them to flee to Medina. Upon this pagan base, Muhammed the Prophet under the inspiration of Allah, achieved something only short of the miraculous in creating a framework within which a whole people turned from multi-idolatry to the inner spiritual devotion directed towards one indivisible God – an all-ruling, all-directing Allah, at the same time very real to the worshipper. It is now to a transformed Kaaba, that Muslims from all over the world make their annual pilgrimage to Mecca.

'Fight in the way of Allah, against those who fight against you, but do not begin hostilities. Allah loveth not aggressors', says the Quran. This may have become the basis for Jehad, Holy War, which many Muslims feel is misinterpreted in western history books, for the spread of Islam has taken place peaceably during recent centuries.

Islam now has a gigantic number of followers. Between one quarter and one fifth of the world's population is Muslim – i.e. more than 650,000,000 people. They are spread over China, Indonesia, Africa and even America and the Caribbean. It is estimated that there are about 1.5 million Muslims in Britain*. Incidentally, the great strength of the Muslim faith is its very sincere and staunch belief in the brotherhood of man without any sense of colour or race. For this reason the highest rate of conversions is amongst Negro populations, both in Africa and the USA. Islam in fact embraces different sociological, climatic, cultural and political conditions. Muslims sometimes retain these strong influences even if of insignificant importance.

For instance, although disapproved, many superstitions still exist at rural level, which do not, in fact, have any sanction in Islamic tenets of faith. Setting out on a journey towards the north on a Tuesday or Wednesday is still considered to be attendant with misfortune and bad luck. The same is thought to be so if a black cat walks across the road at the start of a journey. These are superstitions acquired from a common culture at the village level during the long years of Muslim and Hindu living together in one society, and have become diffused throughout Muslim society, which had its ancestry in the India/Pakistan sub-continent.

It was not until the 10th and 11th centuries AD when regular missionaries were sent out and the Arab traders and travelling Muslims in other countries came into contact with non-Muslims, that a great majority of non-Muslims accepted Islam. The Prophet Muhammed died in the year AD 632 and the spread of Islam after him took place under the rule of political empires, i.e. the Caliphates of Rashidins, Umayyeds, Abbasids and Ottomans. Muslim rule became established in major areas of the world, such as undivided India, Spain, East and South East Asia, and Africa. All over the Muslim world, except for the knowledge of at least the bare essential amount of Arabic used in prayers, the teaching of Islam is carried out in the native vernaculars and abundant literature is available in the major languages of the world.

Muhammed – The Prophet of Islam

Muhammed (May peace be upon Him) was born in August, AD 570 at Mecca, Saudi Arabia. As descendants of Abraham, through Ishmael, the Arabs of those

*Britain 1969 (p.186) an official handbook, COI

days had but a vague idea of the Supreme God. Kaaba, the House of God, was full of idols. The promotion of artistic and scientific knowledge was at a standstill and the people were under the grip of vices such as gambling, drinking of intoxicants, female infanticide, slavery, illegitimate relationships, cheating and inter-tribal strifes. The Arabic language was, however, rich in both prose and poetry, and Arab hospitality was exceptionally good.

Muhammed's father, Abdullah had died even before his birth and his grand-father undertook his upbringing. Muhammed lost his mother at the age of six, his grandfather at the age of eight and was eventually left under the care of an uncle. He was a sensitive young man who was given to wandering off into the desert to fast and meditate. It was under such conditions in fact, that the Archangel Gabriel appeared to him in a vision and cried, 'Recite'.

Thus the Quran came into being. He grew to be a pious man and was recognised as 'El-Ameen' – the Trusty and the Faithful.

Besides the household jobs he used to do for his uncle he was employed as a trade agent by Khadeejah, a wealthy Meccan widow. She received favourable reports of his behaviour and professional knowledge and skill and sent him her offer of marriage. At the age of 25 he married Khadeejah, who was then forty. The marriage was a happy one and she bore him four daughters – Fatima being one of them. At the age of forty Muhammed had a Divine Call to the prophet-hood. The first few who accepted Islam were his wife, Ali, Harris and Abu-Bakr.

The Prophet migrated to Yathrib in the year AD 622 because of opposition in his home town, but a great deal of goodwill was present amongst the inhabitants who had accepted Islam during the pilgrimage to Kaaba. The Meccans tried to harass them even there and a number of battles of great historical significance were fought.

Hijrat – The Beginning of the Muslim Calendar

The flight to Yathrib was known as the Hijrat (flight) and it is from this date, AD 622, that all Muslim calendars are dated. Yathrib was later named Madinath-an-Nabi (City of the Prophet) now known as Medina. Hijrat (the migration of the Prophet from Mecca to Medina) is interpreted as an ever-living reminder to the Muslims that mere geographical ties meant nothing to him.

Muhammed died in the year AD 632 at the age of sixty-three and, though he had married several times, he was left with no male issue. Whoever claims to be his descendant claims it through Fatima and her two sons Hassan and Hussain.

The collection and compilation of the Divine revelations received during 23 years in the form of the Holy Quran was done by Uthman the third Caliph. Muhammed himself had left the outlines for his followers to edit afterwards.

Muhammed was the most excellent example of the embodiment of human and angelic characteristics. The detailed study of his life history establishes this without a doubt. (It is interesting to note that Christ was born of brown com-plexion whereas the descriptions given of Muhammed mention a red and white complexion, with long arched eyebrows divided by a vein which throbbed visibly in moments of passion).

In the words of the well-known historian, Lane-Poole:

'He was of the middle height, rather thin, but broad of shoulders, wide of chest, strong of bone and muscle. His head was massive, strongly developed. Dark hair, slightly curled, flowed in a dense mass down almost to his shoulders. Even in advanced age it was sprinkled by only about twenty grey hairs . . . His face was oval-shaped . . . Great black restless eyes shone out from under long, heavy eyelashes. His nose was large, slightly aquiline – His teeth upon which he bestowed great care, were well set, dazzling white . . . A full beard framed his manly face. His skin was clear and soft, his complexion red and white, his hands were as silk and satin . . . His step was quick and elastic; yet firm and as that of one who steps from a high to low place. In turning his face he would also turn his full body. His whole gait and presence were dignified and imposing. His countenance was mild and pensive His laugh was rarely more than a smile.'

At the time of his death a considerable number of non-Muslims had accepted Islam. These followers like to be called Muslims rather than Muhammedans, because Muhammed at all times wished to make it clear that he was a God-sent prophet, a human being interpreting the Divine Allah, the Beneficent, the Merciful; therefore the religion should not be named after him.

Observance of Islam – Daily Life

A Muslim has a set of systematic rules to order his life. These are known as the Five Pillars of Islam and are described later. This might give rise to the thought that life is governed by rigid laws with ensuing difficulties as Muslims are transferred into alien societies concerned with worldly progress, and the necessary adjustments to industrial and technological demands. But the case is otherwise. A high degree of flexibility exists and so long as the end is based on goodwill the means are quite often immaterial. For example, allowance is made for saying the prayers in the home, or in the open air under certain circumstances, although the Prophet always insisted on saying prayers in the mosque in order to bring to everyone's notice the sense of equality, unity and brotherhood among Muslims.

(a) Interpretation of Religious Injunctions

Within Islam there is little chance, either at the one extreme, of political material-ism taking hold in society or, at the other end, of an other-wordly mystical philosophy becoming part of the individual approach to God.

There are many specific injunctions to what a Muslim must follow in his earthly and daily life and the remarkable thing is that on the whole, no matter where a Muslim finds himself, he will try to ensure that they are carried out in his actual living.

Islam is very definitely opposed to any political 'isms' which are in conflict with the concept of Tawheed (unification of God) and Tawakkul (Trust in God). The concept of Towheed, the principle of Unity, has had a profound effect upon Muslim thought and social ethics. The philosophy which lies behind it is that unity manifests itself in the realm of the natural world. Islam regards the entire cosmos as a unity; it has been created by one God and all its different components are inter-related and they function for the achievement of one purpose – that is to praise the grandeur of God. This singleness of purpose makes the world a moral order.

At the level of society this principle of unity has influenced Muslim thinking more dramatically on the concept of the brotherhood of man. This is no idle term. According to Islam, all human beings form one family. Islam thus refutes the idea of racial superiority, and it is to the eternal credit of Islam that it has quite genuinely and freely lived up to this ideal. Race and colour are of no concern to a Muslim. From the other-worldly point of view the Sufi tradition, although it has had a profound effect on deeply religious Muslims, is not in the majority and is not acceptable to orthodox Muslims. However, among these particular followers of Islam, many men of perfect and absolute authority over religious doctrines have left a lasting influence upon the Arts and Sciences, a dividend for modern thinking in Islamic development.

Saiyedena Hazrat Ghuas-ul-Azam Abu-Mohammed Abdul Qadir (470-561 AH, after the Hijra in AD 622) was a great preacher and exponent of Islamic doctrines as well as being a Sufi mystic. He occupies a unique position among Muslim jurists. He was called, for short, Mohiyuddin, that is Reviver of Religion. He delivered his sermons from a monastery in Baghdad and his principle disciples always heard him from a considerable distance in the outskirts of the city. Once a clergyman, it is said, directed in a dream by Christ to go from the Yemen to meet Hazrat in Baghdad and there accept Islam from his teachings, declared his dream at one of the assemblies in that city to prove Hazrat's high rank among mystics.

Whether a layman would understand this cannot be vouched but the spiritual-istic side of the Muslim faith is for those who have the calling and the sensitivity for it, just as in any other faith. Sir Oliver Lodge writes in his book *The Reality of a Spiritual World* (page 12): 'The basic conclusion to which I have been led, is that a spiritual world is a reality, that there are many orders and grades of being, that the human spirit continues, that there is no inseparable barrier between different orders of existence and that under certain conditions intercommunion is possible'. These words acknowledge what most mystics feel, a unity of faith in God the One. This is universally acknowledged as true. But for life in the ordinary day to day affairs, and for the practical purposes of the laymen, the interpretation of the Quran and Hadith are grouped into the following grades:

1. Obligatory; such as the Five Pillars of Islam

2. Recommended but not obligatory; such as hospitality to strangers and kindness to neighbours

3. Indifferent; towards the looking after family pets such as cats

4. Disapproved but not forbidden; divorce

5. Prohibited; drinking of alchohol and eating pork meat

41

(b) Fundamentals of Islam

Different schools of Fiqah (Islamic jurisprudence) have developed because of differing interpretations and explanations of the Quran and the Hadith. The categorising and grouping of these ordinances has brought about a major division into two sects in Islam, the Shias and the Sunnis. This is much the same as has happened in other religions which are equally rich in doctrinal and theological principles.

The Quran is not a work of voluminous size, but it definitely describes in more detail than any other religious Holy Book, the essential points and details of life that have to be maintained and honoured. Those matters which have been omitted and which could not have been included due to the changing circumstances of life which arise from scientific and technological development (birth control, for instance), are dealt with after agreed mutual consultations based upon equitable and non-controversial judgments, and within the framework of the Quran and the Hadith.

There is the exemplary story, for instance, of Muaz. Muhammed appointed him Qazi of Yemen (Justice of the Peace) and asked him about his criteria for giving judgments. Muaz said that he would look into the Quran for it and if he failed to find a precedent there, he would look in the Hadith. If he failed even there he would then exercise his own judgment. Muhammed approved of this.

All new problems have been tackled upon such lines. During the passage of historical time different schools of jurisprudence developed – Hanafi, Maliki, Shaafei and Hambli (all four follow the Sunni persuasion).

The great Imams (religious leaders) of Sunni, Shia and other sects are equally revered and their interpretations of the Quran and the Hadith remain fundamentally the same, only differing at certain stages, but not violently.

Muslims from Islamic states who have been transplanted into Christian surroundings will naturally stick fervently to their own religious persuasion but at the same time will be inclined to hammer out some of the cultural disparities subject of course to the proper safeguard of their ethical codes.

Local authority departments and even private individuals in places where overseas populations concentrate and where multiple religious denominations now exist, have an uphill task in understanding the opposing views sometimes put forward to the same problem, and in finding a satisfactory solution without offending any one section of these communities, as well as the host community.

It is difficult for the British to comprehend the subtleties of difference *within* the Asian or West Indian communities – but they are there as they are even in the most homogeneous society. It is very easy to put all Pakistanis, all Indians in a category and to label them as one, but there are differences of opinion even among themselves. The best thing in the circumstances is to elicit the views of a cross-section of the orthodox members of the immigrant community because these are the people who can explain the pattern of living as experienced in the country of origin, and the problems of adjustment that arise under new conditions. They can act as a channel of communication between the host and Muslim community, because they know the relationship of Islamic law to everyday life even in this country. Not all official interpreters used by local authority and police are necessarily competent. They may be more attuned to the British way of life than their own, and fail to relate the problems and pressures of the incoming village communities whose religious requirements demand a more orthodox outlook, which they themselves have relinquished long ago.

Muslim immigrants (practising or non-practising) all have at least to believe in a number of fundamental principles of Islam which are the hallmark of the Muslim. These are known as the Five Tenets of FAITH. The answer to such questions as how many of them practice them, or how far do they practice them is subject to many factors. The strange environment and the struggle to fit into it, or even to surpass the others in a changing mode of life naturally disorientate some members. Many of the men are alone and far away from their families. But such factors are only marginal and do not influence a devout Muslim who would practice the following in his own humble way.

THE FIVE PILLARS OF FAITH

1. Faith in Allah

Proclamation of belief in one God. His Prophets, His Books, Angels, and Destiny (that God ordains events) and resurrection after death.

Whoever proclaims with real reverence: 'Laa-ilaaha il-lal-lah; muhammad rasoo-lul-laah' – There is no God but Allah; Muhammed is his Messenger! – that person is a Muslim . . . This Arabic formula is termed as Kalimah irrespective of time and place. It is a common and repeated utterance from a Muslim of any understanding of his faith.

Kalimah
The world of Islam today consists of individuals, families, tribes, races, nations and states. Every nation is possessed with the idea of nationalism and one nation has been a threat to the peace of another. It has been impossible to maintain unity or brotherhood. Moreover no one nation has ever enjoyed territorial or linguistic homogeneity and 'peace has, therefore, been a short interlude between wars in the history of mankind'. So rightly commented Sir Winston Churchill. The proclamation of Kalimah insists on one God and one Prophet and the nationalism is defined in the Quranic verse as 'Humanity has made one single nation'. This idealistic universal brotherhood is realised through the common ideology – The Holy Quran.

The Kalimah rejects political sovereignty of man and instead confirms God's superiority. In recent years dishonest ruling hands have made it a fast-fading reality. Under the inspiration of Kalimah the human mind endeavours to coincide the law with morality and to approach in material terms the highest office in the state (which used to be called Caliphate – the vice-regency of God on Earth.) One of these Caliphates came into the possession of Caliph Umar who obeyed the commands of the Quran to the full and flogged to death his

43

son who had committed adultery. According to the Quran 'each party to the fornication must be flogged with hundred stripes'.

The Kalimah divests a man of the idea of ownership and inculcates in him the habit of sharing his extra wealth with others. Thus the idea of almsgiving, Khairaat and Zakāt came into existence. It discourages hatred and prejudice.

In the heyday of Islam, Kalimah created a culture based on simple living, equal participation of effort, and a general reaping of benefits for the whole of society. The cultures of imperial Arabs of Damascus and Cordova, the Turkish Emperors, the Great Moghul Kings of India were Muslim cultures which lacked the simplicity of prophet Muhammed's teaching. They were tinged with personal grandeur and the idea of fame in posterity. In the philosophy of Kalimah art and sciences must promote knowledge, goodness and eradicate poverty, ignorance and disease. Abdul Qadir Jilani, Ibne-Khalddin, Ibne-Sina and Ibne-Hayan were the jurist, mathematician, physician and chemist who undertook the task to reveal and uphold the limitless version of the Kalimah. The philosophy of life based exclusively on the meanings of the Kalimah helped Abdul Qadir Jilani to explore forty different explanations of a certain Quranic verse. Thus he showed the dynamic nature of the Holy Quran.

2. Prayers of a Certain Order to be said Five Times a Day

This is the first sura, which has been called 'the essence of the Quran', the Lord's Prayer of Islam.

In the name of Allah, the Beneficent, the Merciful!
Praise be to Allah, Lord of the Worlds,
               the Beneficent, the Merciful,

Ruler of the Day of Judgment,
Thee alone we worship; thee alone we ask for help.
Show us the straight path,
The path of those whom Thou has favoured;
Not of those who have earned Thine anger
             nor of those who go astray.

3. Almsgiving for Charity – Zakāt

A share of each Muslim's savings, $2\frac{1}{2}$ per cent. is ordered to go anonymously towards the support of the poor and for the religious education of students in the mosque and the cultural teaching of children (such as happens in Britain in order that they retain their own language).

The principle of Zakāt provides the basis for the conception of a Muslim Welfare State. Hoarding of money at the cost of others' suffering is contrary to the Islamic spirit. One example is on record of Muhammed's economist companion, Abu-Zarr Ghaffari, who used to stand on the crossroads of Mecca and ask for money from passers-by for the public treasury.

The fact that the interest drawn on $2\frac{1}{2}$ per cent. of a Muslim's savings is given away as alms or Zakāt might genuinely compel this man to ask the Inland Revenue for the income tax rebate on this part of his earnings. In fact some Muslims in Britain remit the interest on savings in English banks to relatives in Pakistan for distribution to the poor. There is a month of the lunar year named Zakāt when assessment is made for this purpose.

4. **Fasting for One Full Lunar Month**

A moveable commemoration, called Ramadhan, at which the Prophet is be-lieved to have received the first revelations from the Angel Gabriel. The fast is from dawn to dusk daily.

The month of Ramadhan is very sacred to a Muslim – first, because the revelation to Muhammed was completed in this month, secondly, in the last third of this lunar month there falls a night called Leila-tul-Qadar when prayers are met with an exceedingly great kindness by Allah, and, thirdly, the final reckoning upon all those who are born or die in the year takes place.

5. **Performance of Pilgrimage known as Hadj to Holy Places especially Mecca and Medina**

This should be made at least once in a lifetime, if it can be afforded, to kiss the Black Meteorite, the shrine and sanctuary of Allah, which has to be walked around seven times.

The social impact of massive gatherings of people of all classes, colour, education, tongues and cultures in the one place of pilgrimage for some length of time is no less profitable in inculcating the idea of universal brotherhood, than the spiritual doctrine as taught in the Quran. This points to the fact that religion and politics in Islam go hand in hand.

(c) Early Life, and Social Customs which are binding for Muslims in Britain

Birth

The overall Muslim population is on the increase throughout the world through birth or conversions. The new-born baby, soon after its birth, listens to the 'Call to Prayer', the Arabic text and transcription of which is known to almost all Muslims. Those who wish to be converted take a bath and toilet ablutions and say a special prayer in the presence of two witnesses. The shaving of a baby's head at birth is common, a symbolic act to take away the uncleanliness of birth, as well as to help the hair grow in greater profusion.

Names

Muslim names are usually the combination and permutation of the ninety-nine names of Muhammed the Prophet and of Allah, each meaning a different and principle attribute.

Those teachers concerned with Muslim children might find it convenient for remembering their names by writing down all the names of an individual and then grading them according to the usual requirements. It is no good asking for their 'Christian' names. That will not be understood and is anyway an anomaly. Their first names are best called common names and can be supplemented by father's names, dates of birth, and addresses to make them more certain.

Every Muslim has a tribal name based on the name of the area from which he has come, or from the founder of the clan. This is the equivalent of a surname. If this could be accepted as such it may solve some of the confusions which arise from too many Alis and Khans, and for local authority departments, and hospital and police records.

For instance a young man may state his name as Abdullah. This is how he is known in Pakistan. His full name however may be Abdullah Haroon which is a name derived from the famous Muslim Caliph Haroon or he may be known as Mohammed Yunus (the equivalent of John Smith). In this case his father's name can be added, such as Mohammed Yunus, son of Hayat Khan (whose name again corresponds to John Smith!). The word Khan constantly causes confusion. It is not a surname in the western sense. Khan means the head of a tribe, such as Khan Abdul Ghaffar Khan. The first is the title, and the latter is part of the name but *not* the surname.

Circumcision

Circumcision is obligatory for a male Muslim child. No age is fixed. It can be at any time before the age of eight. To avoid any subsequent difficulty it can be syncronised with the removal of the baby's umbilical cord scar seven or eight days after the birth. In Britain, if a Muslim doctor is not available there are difficulties as sometimes excessive amounts have been charged (in a few cases £50-£60 for the simple operation). In the Jewish community an overall charge of £5 is made, as this is not done under the Health Service. Perhaps this matter can be investigated or Pakistani doctors can perform the simple operation as a community service for their own people, as Jewish doctors have done.

Sacrifice

The Hadj, pilgrimage to Mecca, and the Zakāt, the tax on one's savings in kind or cash, have definite and concise rules to follow in their execution. Sacrifice of a goat or sheep is again obligatory and is performed by those who can afford it on the eve of Eid-ul-Adha. Muslims in this country have been observed performing this duty through help from their dependents in the country of emigration. Anyone who wishes to carry it out over here will of course follow the rules of the Local Health Department.

Money Matters

Whereas insurance of life and property with Government bodies and individual societies is allowed, games of chance and speculation are forbidden. Loans of money are offered to friends without interest. In Pakistan interest from banks is utilised for community development projects or given as alms to the poor but here, for fear that unclaimed interest from money deposited in banks may be donated to schemes opposed to the cause of Islam, interest has been realised even though it is not one of the principles of Muslim faith to accept interest on money.

A loan can be extended to the needy but without interest, to be returned at the borrower's convenience. Investment of wealth in commercial terms is encouraged provided certain principles such as reasonable profits, proper weights and measures and correct terms and conditions in the case of joint enterprises (laid down beforehand) are adhered to.

(d)   General Habits

Christopher Dawson, writing in *The Dynamics of World History*, has said: 'Islam is at once a culture and a religion in which culture can hardly be conceived of as existing apart from religion'.

Fasting

A fasting Muslim, a slim man who could, clearly, get no slimmer than he actually was, had to explain to an inquisitive British colleague the spiritual benefits gained by fasting. It was, indeed, difficult for him to communicate to the questioner the sharp and subtle improvement acquired in the qualities of toler-ance, patience, self-control, resistance to temptation – and even the pleasure experienced in the sacrifice of physical desires. This kind of thing, perhaps, is difficult even for an ascetic to explain clearly without having performed a miracle, and especially in a secular atmosphere where the concept behind fasting is now no longer familiar, and where self-discipline is not held at a premium.

On the other hand, one could observe a fasting immigrant child showing signs of listlessness because of his hunger and could, in consequence, conclude that the fasting was having an adverse effect. The question arises, as to whether such children are compelled to fast without knowing the reason. Are the benefits accruing from fasting adequately explained to them? Do immigrant parents themselves know the importance and significance of fasting or even the funda-mental injunctions of Islam for that purpose? These are matters of some difficulty in view of the complex nature of the situation and the subject and the relatively poor education of many of the parents who have come to Britain from entirely rural backgrounds. This is more a social and educational problem than a religious one.

Eating

By British Law, it is an offence to keep live chickens in the house. It has, however, been a common practice with Indo-Pakistan immigrants. There is, of course, no religious ordinance which would lead people to break the law in this respect. In fact, the meat of any kind of animal slaughtered ritually is available from Indian and Pakistani grocers and butchers and a prompt inquiry from immigrant associations and voluntary organisations can help to stop ill-practices of this kind which are of a behaviouristic rather than religious nature. Much is the result of blind custom rather than intelligent understanding of faith.

Pork and alcoholic drinks are forbidden. Other kinds of meat are the same for Muslims as for Christians, except that there is a difference in the way in which the animals must be killed. The ritual of slaughtering is performed by pronouncing the formula beginning with Bismillah (with the name of God) and cutting the throat at one clean stroke on the respiratory tube, the stomach tube and the two big jugular veins and carotid arteries not touching the spinal column, much less severing the head or stunning the animal. The blood should be drained out straight away. There remain such questions as to how Muslims make up their protein difficiences if they can't get meat which is not ritually killed. It could be, of course, that they forget about such things as 'protein resources' and 'metaboism' and 'protein synthesis'.

Pork Meats
There are strong reasons of hygiene behind the forbidding of pork meats of any kind for human consumption. Zoologically, pigs, rats and man are subject to a lethal disease caused by the trichina worm. Man can pick up trichinosis from eating poorly cooked pork when pigs have eaten infected rats or raw refuse. Cysts in the muscles of the pig, when eaten, can reproduce in the human intestine and the larvae, then bore their way into the blood stream – this can eventually cause severe pain, paralysis and even death. One has to remember again the conditions of Arabia at the time of Muhammed and the fact that modern methods of curing pork did not exist. The intense heat of the desert made such a strict injunction so long-lasting. The Asian systems of medicine – both Muslim Unani and Hindu Ayurvedic – lay great stress upon the effects of diet, not only to bodily health but to mental personality.

Among Muslims the pig is regarded as a dirty animal, and the common theory is that human beings take on the tendencies of the foodstuffs that they may eat to extremes. This is noticeable in heavy meat eaters who tend to look gross. Moreover modern research has disclosed that pork meat is more likely to increase the cholesterol deposits in the human arteries and hence influence hypertension more than any other kind of meat.

Similarly alcholic drinks are also forbidden. Gold and silver utensils as food containers and service are again forbidden, because this is like hoarding wealth that could instead go to the poor. Leading a simple life is much stressed by Muhammed who once showed his disapproval when he saw his wife wearing silken embroidered cloth.

The Quran says: 'Forbidden unto you (for food) are carrion, and blood and swine flesh, and that which hath been dedicated unto another than God, and the strangled, and the dead through beating, and the dead through falling from a height and that which hath been killed by the goring of horns, saving that which ye make lawful by the death stroke of slaughtering and that which hath been immolated into idols, but whoever is forced by hunger, not by will, to sin, for him lo! God is forgiving, merciful'.

Because all Muslims are enjoined not to kill, slaughter of animals must be taken in the name of God, Bismillah.

Dress

In dress habits women are told to avoid all that is characteristic of the glamour girl. Dress should cover all the parts of the body and should not help to define physical features. In consequence, the anglicising of women so far as dress is concerned is unlikely to occur. Use of cloth made entirely of silk and garments of red colour, are discouraged also. This has given rise to the passionate feelings felt by some Pakistani parents concerning the dress for their teenage daughters in schools, for P.E. lessons and in mixed swimming classes.

Hardly a day passes when one doesn't hear or read about a head teacher insisting on English dress from his/her Muslim girl students in the school. Sometimes it results in wasting the useful time of the pupil during this conflict between the teacher and the parents, especially when the latter take the law in their own hands and keep daughters away from school. The Press makes use of such happenings and people interpret this as 'immigrants not conforming to English ways of life'. Issues become confused, and the immigrants are made a sort of scapegoat for political reasons and not educational ones. The workable solution arrived at by a number of Local Education Authorities is the prescription of a uniform different from English dress but suitable for religious observances. In fact in a number of schools the white trousers are worn with tunics or kameez made by girls in the needlework classes to a regulation pattern. The Muslim girls have generally been doing P.E. in slacks; separate swimming rotas have been chalked out for girls. At certain places the Muslim girls of secondary age are exempted from swimming if the parents wish it.

Social 'brushing up' in educational reception centres of the new arrivals from overseas prevents a lot of trouble in later school life. This normally consists of training in the use of toilets, road safety, essential requirements of the English school system of education and examinations, school dinners, welfare and health of school children. This is much the same as for the adults. There are problems attached to the delivery of these instructions, especially when the teacher in charge is English and the children have only scanty knowledge of the English language. Some of the problems are religious ones, e.g. a Muslim child refuses to eat any kind of meat. An idea worth trying is to include some Indian and Pakistani dishes and savouries in the menu. Muslim children would love grilled and chopped meat (except pork) killed ritually and obtained from the Pakistani shopkeepers in the town.

Greetings and Arabic Formulas

There are many common brief formulas, most of them in Arabic, which a careful Muslim would always say impromptu when alone or in the company of men and women. He would always pronounce 'Bismil-laah' (with the name of God) at the beginning of an action and 'Alhumdu-lil-laah' (Praise be to God) at the end. There is a general feeling among those of simple faith that each good or bad happening is the will of God Almighty.

When something is promised in the future a Muslim always says Inshal-laah (if God be willing) and greets a person by saying 'Assalm-o-Alaikum' (Peace be on you). That person in turn greets him: 'Wa-alaikum-us-salaam' (and peace be on you). Muslims have 'sayings' for various occasions. After sneezing, for instance, they say 'Alhumdu-lil-laah' for having done so successfully and 'sorry' to recompense the disturbance caused to others nearby! One who hears some-body sneezing says 'Yar Hammdul-illah' – May God bless you.

The right hand is used for handling good and clean jobs and things, while the left is used for dirty jobs. This is also true within the Indian tradition, the left hand being used for personal ablutions. When entering a house one steps in the door by using the right foot and when leaving it steps out with the left foot.

'Cleanliness is half of the faith' is one of Muhammed's sayings and is observed rigorously. Taking a bath becomes imperative after cohabitation, wet dreams, menses, the time the blood flow stops after child birth and always before the large Friday prayers. The process of bath and ablution involves the removing of traces of dirt or undesirable material on the body. A shower bath is best suited to this purpose rather than lying in one's own dirty water in a bath. Public baths for this reason have always been under much discussion. Paper alone has never been found sufficient in the W.C. Floor toilets without pedestals, with handy approach to a water tap are missed very badly in the West. Some employers of Asian labour have provided these facilities, Bradford Transport Corporation, for example.

(e) Daily and Funeral Prayers

For daily prayers the requirements needed are any clean piece of land and the ability to stand with face towards Kaaba in Mecca, clean dress and water for ablutions. The routine five prayers – one in the morning, two in the afternoon, one at sunset and one about two hours after sunset during the day – are obligatory.

In case of shortage of time, travelling and sickness these prayers can be shortened and even postponed. There are some, however, who would say the prayers at the right time and would never postpone them.

A Muslim on his death bed pronounces (if he can) the formula: 'There is no God if not God himself. Muhammed is The Messenger of God'.

The dead body is given a bath before burial which is preceded by the saying of funeral prayers. This is again governed by certain rules – such as the time, the kind of person leading the prayer, etc. The service can be performed in the absence of the body which might receive burial elsewhere in the world. The dead body is buried in such a way that the grave is dug parallel to Mecca and the face is turned towards it. Lavish spending on graves is not recommended. Muslims resident in Britain often send the corpses back home for burial (the cost being approximately £140) for a number of reasons. The religious one (in addition to those based purely on sentiment) is to bury the relative in a big graveyard that always visited by pious men praying for the dead in the life hereafter and for forgiveness of sins. This is also the reason why Muslims ask for a separate graveyard here in some towns in Britain.

50

The System of Morality – Muslim Women

'Respect for Women' is an essential teaching of Islam. 'I advise you to be good to women', Muhammed said to the Muslims many times. Fatima, Muhammed's daughter, well known amongst Muslims as the 'Lady of Paradise' and 'Lady of Light', is an embodiment of divine qualities. Besides her, many more saintly women like Rabia in the past commanded respect from the masses.

The ancient Babylonians, Assyrians, Persians, Israelites before the time of Moses, Syro-phonecian races, Athenians and even high caste Brahmins all exercised polygamy. On the other hand Spartan females usually had more than one husband. As society advanced monogamy generally comes into practice. The analysis of the position of women folk in Muslim society has been ambiguous and many Christian observers have been bewildered by the social behaviour of Muslim men to women.

The relevant Quranic passages in connection with marriages are: 'You may marry two, three or four wives but not more', and 'if you cannot deal equitably and justly with all you shall marry only one'. In the light of these statements plurality of wives is made a controversial point. Nevertheless the word 'equity' to wives (never overlooked by the great Muslim thinkers) has helped the legislator in almost every Muslim state to abolish polygamy except in cases where the first wife is established as barren or that she cannot bring forth a male issue. Due to lack of education and social attitudes it is difficult to establish that male sterility may be the cause of infertility also.

Marriage is, according to Islam, a bilateral *social contract*. The parents certainly aid in this by their counsel and their experience in searching or selecting for the right life companion, looking into the whole family background and heredity, but the couple should have the last say in the matter. Illegal practices may exist from region to region and class to class, but the law does not recognise the customs which contravene its provisions and much is being done in Pakistan to eliminate plurality of wives.

Annulment also exists in Muslim law both for husband and wife. The court of justice also possesses the right of separation of the couple on the plaint of the wife if the husband is incapable of fulfilling his conjugal duties, or if he is suffering from a particularly serious sickness or if he disappears for years without leaving a trace.

The fact that a Muslim has more than one wife does not mean he can claim the benefits from the National Insurance Schemes for all the wives although *all* children can receive family allowances. However this applies in British society for children born out of wedlock. It is generally accepted that the first marriage, the legal one under British law, is the one to which income tax, maintenance laws, social welfare benefits, etc, applies. It is the first wife who by law is the 'informant' in case of death of a Muslim husband.

Men who ignore their wives and do not take them into their confidence or who do them an injustice such as beating or confining them if the wives disagree with them, or advance an opinion of their own and impose on them what God has not asked, manifest sheer ignorance of the Quranic right and duties of women,

51

and need thorough reorientation of their unhealthy conduct and ideas, but this is a matter of social progress at the village level, rather than religious backwardness.

A Muslim seen with his wife walking three steps behind in the rear either falls in this category, or has a physically unhealthy woman following him!

Romans usually debated whether woman was a 'person' or 'thing' when Muhammed declared 'women are but sisters of men'. Women were not allowed to touch the Bible when Lady Hafsa at Medina held the Quranic manuscripts in her trust. Time has changed and the Western women now have far more emancipation amongst them than those from the East. Education is the greatest measure in judging what is good and what is bad, but those with little formal education suffer a great impact from the full force of Western films and television. Women cannot be forbidden to watch TV. The implications and temptations of viewing some programmes can well be imagined.

In view of all this, youth committees should not be surprised if very small numbers of Muslim girls or none at all attend the Civic Youth Clubs. Visits to the clubs, Muslim parents believe, will result in free mixing of girls and boys, leading to immorality. How far they would exercise and impose their views on their children depends on a number of factors such as the education at home, and shool and society, etc.

The matter of dress habit again depends on standards of morality and modesty amongst the women of each race. All veiled women are not morally sound, nor bare-legged women immoral and vice versa. The absorption of minority groups sociologically is bound to occur but the thorough study of his religion would tell an individual when he has overstepped his religious principles in observance. The Shalwar or Sari, for example, is a typical woman's dress, which meets the religious as well as social sanctions. If, however, a Shalwar or Sari helps a woman to emphasise her body rather than disguise it, then she really needs some other suitable dress.

Birth Control

The issue of birth control which necessarily means the prevention of conception and hence the procreation of children is rather difficult to be answered from the Quran or the traditions of the Prophet which include no precedent of this kind.

In view of infanticide abortion and other means of getting rid of unwanted children that went on in Arabia before the advent of Islam, the Quran however contains this narration to stop such ill-practices: 'Do not kill your children for fear of poverty. We will provide for them and for you'. In the circumstances the modern Muslims have adjudged the pros and cons of the issue of birth control using their own discretion.

The general principle has been pointed out in the Quran time and again to weigh the good and evil of a habit and then decide accordingly. While prohibiting the use of alcoholic drinks, for example, the Quran continues to say . . . 'Its sin and evil far outweigh its benefits'. The factors such as the health of mothers, the effects of heredity, social and economic imbalance, which are some of the dangers in the growth of population of a country, if they are taken into account in detail, seem to be groundless and God's promise mentioned above, appears to hold good even now and after. Material gains in scientific and technological advancement, the mineral wealth contained in the unexplored lands like the Amazon's basin, Iceland's plains, arable Alaska and the fertile Arctic regions that abound, this vast wealth for human consumption is some of the evidence to support His promise. The immense sources of wealth which the Creator has placed at the disposal of man as a result of his increasing innate habit of exploration meet the demands of our subsistence. All Malthusian fears are unreal and all geographical fetters shattered when one sees the American farmer producing wheat to feed the Indian famine-stricken and OXFAM despatching ship-loads of medicines to the disease-afflicted millions of Africans.

The intellectually sound and theologically well-informed Muslim believes that the sole aim of sexual intercourse is procreative rather than recreative. A prominent Muslim scholar, Maulana Sayyid Abul Ala Maududi, thinks efforts should be geared to explore more land and resources than to inhibit the growth of humankind. Nevertheless the population of Pakistan is growing at a normal pace because of the Family Planning Commission set up by the Government which is working in this field despite the differing views of the people. The loop method is said to have worked well there. Whosoever resists the suggestion on birth control is free to do so and no compulsion is laid down on the family.

The immigrant family after a year of its arrival in this country increases its number of children partly because of long separation and partly because of the small number of the family and the feeling that one more would not be of much burden. The Muslim immigrant family must be well aware of the religious views on birth control, but presumably would listen to the advice from the Health Department in order to better the children's prospects and their own economic wellbeing as a smaller, more manageable family.

When it has been necessary for a male doctor to carry out a medical examination, the Muslim ladies have often been reluctant to undress. If no lady doctor is available (a great asset to any Local Authority where Asians have settled in some numbers) it will not be a sin according to her religion to expose any part of her body that a male doctor wishes to examine. It may be harmful for her or for the baby in her womb, if she is an expectant mother, if a proper medical examination is not made possible because of her unwillingness to take her clothes off. There have been several cases where Pakistan ladies have died in hospital rather than allow themselves to be examined. Again this is a question of social education among people of very orthodox rural background.

Principle Festivals and Timetable for Future Lunar Reckoning
The two principle feasts which occupy a great religious as well as a social importance to a Muslim are the breaking of the fast at the end of the month of Ramadhan and the sacrifice of the pilgrimage. All kinds of work in the Muslim world cease on these two days, known as Eid-ul-Fitr and Eid-ul-Adha respectively. Muslim workers will naturally stay away from work if not given an

authorised holiday, and some children (as Jewish children already do for their festivals) will miss school at least in the mornings to attend the large prayers and sermons in the mosque.

Eid-ul-Fitr is held on the first day of the month of Shawal and marks the end of the long month of fasting. On this great day of celebration people get up early in the morning, take a bath, say regular morning prayers due every day before sunrise, eat dates or other sweets, and having put on new or clean clothes, set off for the biggest mosque in the town. There they say full prayers which are held soon after sunrise.

Every well-to-do person is meant to give alms to the poor on this day, preferably before the prayers. Detailed standards are laid down for the amount of alms and the eligibility of the receiving persons.

At the end of prayers people usually pronounce Eid greetings and embrace one another to fulfil the Prophet's example. They enjoy a sumptuous midday meal and it is a day of happiness. Even in this country the atmosphere of rejoicing is not lost and Eid cards are even sent to, and received from, British friends. In Muslim countries great fairs are held in the villages, young men gather for folk dancing to the insistent rhythms of large drums, children sing songs and the village elders arrange native-style horse races and wrestling.

Eid-ul-Adha is held on the tenth day of the month of Dhul-Hijja, marking the end of the ceremonies of the pilgrimage of Ibrahim and the sacrifice of Ishmael. It is the second great festival of the Muslim calendar which is celebrated to remind Muslims that one should not hesitate to sacrifice anything for the glory of God. Prayers and other rituals are much the same as the earlier Eid but instead of giving alms, the sacrifice of an animal (usually a goat or lamb) is made obligatory. This can be put into practice during any of the three days (excluding night time) beginning with the day of Eid.

Details are again set out for the type of animal sacrifice, the disposal, and the distribution of the meat to those in need, etc. This Eid also provides a chance for a great gathering of relatives, fun and amusements, and feasts for all.

There are a number of other festivals such as the Prophet Mohammed's Birthday (Eid-milad-un-Nabi) which falls on the twelth of the month of Rabi-ul-Auwal, three months after the Eid of Sacrifice,and Muhurram. These are public holidays in Pakistan.

Muhurram

Another festival – Muhurram – commemorates the battle and death of Hussain, the grandson of the Prophet, and the imprisonment of his family during the contest for the succession of the Sixth Caliphate. The tenth day of this month, which is also called Muhurram, goes even further back in time to the date of the drowning and death of Pharoah and his army in the river Nile while chasing Prophet Moses and his followers. In gratefulness to this, the Prophet fasted on this day, as do Jews now to commemorate this historic event.

Muhammed also directed Muslims to fast on this day and also on the 9th and 10th of Muhurram.

Forty years after the death of the Prophet Muhammed during the Caliphate of Yazid, Hussain, his grandson, was killed on the same day. All Muslims know it and every year at the beginning of this month they recite the Holy Quran for the good of his departed soul. The Shia sect especially who trace their lineage from Hussain's side of the family, celebrate this day although all Muslims believe in the historical truth of why the battle was fought.

The Shias mourn his death for 40 days and meetings are held in the evenings for the first nine days to recall the incidents especially for the benefit of the younger ones. A mourning procession takes place on the tenth day with large 'tazias' or floats, and with the chanting of religious hymns and ballads. Some of the participants are so moved that tears stream down their faces, and they flagellate their own bodies to 'suffer' along with Hussain. No weddings, TV shows or musical recordings take place around this time. For the English dates of these festivals see the following chart.

The Hijri lunar year is 10-11 days shorter than the solar year (354-355 days). Seventy-one days after 1st of the month of Muharram (the First new year day) is the Prophet's Day, then after 166 days is followed by the fasting month of Ramadhan (29 or 30 days), the end of which is Eid-ul-Fitr.

Two hundred and sixty four days after the Prophet's Day is Eid-ul-Adha. This table may be useful for those managements employing predominantly Pakistani labour forces because of the difficulty encountered with managements who remain adamant in not giving leave of absence for principal festivals already long-established in other religious communities. On the other hand further notice needs to be given by Muslim associations so that managements know well in advance, and not the day before a Festival so that the matter can be settled equitably.

Hijri Year	1st Muharram	Prophet's Day	1st Ramadhan	Eid-ul-Adha
1388	30 Mar 68	9 June 68	22 Nov 68	28 Feb 69
1389	19 Mar 69	29 May 69	11 Nov 69	17 Feb 70
1390	8 Mar 70	18 May 70	31 Oct 70	9 Feb 71
1391	26 Feb 71	6 May 71	21 Oct 71	27 Jan 72
1392	15 Feb 72	26 Apr 72	9 Oct 72	15 Jan 73
1393	3 Feb 73	15 Apr 73	28 Sept 73	4 Jan 74
1394	24 Jan 74	5 Apr 74	18 Sept 74	26 Dec 74
1395	13 Jan 75	25 Mar 75	9 Sept 75	14 Dec 75
1396	3 Jan 76	13 Mar 76	26 Aug 76	2 Dec 76
1397	22 Dec 76	2 Mar 77	16 Aug 77	22 Nov 77
1398	11 Dec 77	20 Feb 78	5 Aug 78	11 Nov 78
1399	1 Dec 78	10 Feb 79	26 July 79	1 Nov 79
1400	20 Nov 79	30 Jan 80	14 July 80	20 Oct 80

A difference of a day on either side of the dates given above can be taken into account subject to the appearance of moon. All Muslim festivals are subject to the phases of the moon, and have to take into account the 'siting' of the new moon as it is called. This in fact means the actual 'sighting' of the new moon, sometimes impossible in the English climate with low cloud base – therefore Muslim religious leaders confirm this by telephoning religious institutions based in Muslim countries where the new moon would have been sighted.

Some Islamic Views

Art

The Prophet did not appreciate portrait drawings but with the times the attitude of the people has changed. However, drawing of the Prophet's profile can even now cause a great row. Muslims have, however, selectively contributed in the field of mosaics and murals and fine works of tracery and floral embellishment. Al-hambra (Spain) and Taj Mahal (India) are the living examples of these. This may affect children's attitude to figure drawing. It is best to start a hesitant immigrant child at school with patterns, and floral designs which they are naturally skilled at designing.

Music

The practice of singing without musical instruments is very vague. Only very devout Muslims have abandoned instruments when singing. The children's parents will, of course, object to their children attending religious assembly at school if they think they are being converted to Christianity, and hearing Christian religious hymns.

Religious Education in Schools

If some universal truths contained in the Quran and also other Holy Books could be made use of once or twice a week the children from all religious faiths would surely join with English children in morning prayers. In places of dense Muslim concentrations of population, their children attend the local mosques for prayers and learning of their religion and language, (Arabic, Urdu or Bengali) during the week and at weekends. The number of hours spent each week at the mosque by typical Muslim children varies from four to six; there are some extreme cases of those who never visit the mosque at all, and on the other hand of those who spend as many as twelve hours there. The education of children in state schools coupled with study in the mosques satisfies the aspiration of Muslim parents.

So long as the child complies with the school regulations and requirements and so long as his parents understand that he will have to compete with native children when trying to achieve his ambitions after school in finding a decent job, no one can really interfere. After all English parents decide how many hours their children will spend watching television.

The immigrant child, if he attends the mosque, will have his attitude to Christianity influenced to some extent by his Muslim teachers and his attitudes to his own religion will be influenced by his knowledge of Christianity. These children might appear to be over-worked but invaluable social education imparted at the mosque has helped the English teacher administratively in many ways. The religious leader of the community can well be a bridge between the school head and Muslim parents in cases of difficulty.

56

Some teachers in this modern age are of the view that children should not receive any religious instruction. To a Muslim this has dangers – in that the child may become more a moralist with his attentions self-centred on humanity, rather than a religionist with attentions centred on God. Muslim parents will always guide their children and the religious instruction in the mosque will always be intensified when the effect of one society upon the other is experienced. Every Muslim parent knows what the Prophet says: 'Every child is born in accord with Divine Nature, it is his parents who make of him a Jew, a Zoroastrian or a Christian'. This implies that every baby is born a Muslim (unless otherwise directed by its parents) and therefore Muslim parents have a singular duty to reinforce the teachings of Islam. Instead of demanding blind acceptance educated Muslims are beseeched in the Holy Quran to use reason in understanding the truth and to investigate the natural phenomena in order to realise the word of God in the works of God and to harness natural forces for the realisation of human destiny under the overall direction of the Vice-regency of God.

Iqbal, the philosopher poet of Islam, visualises the place of religion in life more effectively in his lectures on the reconstruction of religious thought in Islam and exhorts to bring about thorough changes in the education of Muslim children in accordance with true religious spirit. 'Experience shows', he maintains, 'that truth revealed through pure reason is incapable of bringing that fire of living conviction which personal revelation alone can bring. That is the reason why pure thought has so little influenced men, while religion has always elevated individuals and transformed whole societies.'

Even in the modern age in connection with the necessity of religious education, he reasoned: 'Religion, which in its higher manifestation is neither dogma nor priesthood nor ritual, can alone prepare modern man for the burden of the great responsibility which the advancement of modern science necessarily involves, and restore to him that attitude of faith which makes him capable of winning a personality here and retaining it hereafter. It is only by raising to a fresh vision of his origin and future his whence and wither that man will eventually triumph over a society motivated by an inhuman competition and a civilisation which has lost its spiritual unity by an inner conflict of religious and political values'.

His conception of Islamic education both in form and content (as is apparent from his poetry) is the one that refuses the acquisition of passive knowledge, but accepts the one that encourages self-knowledge, develops an all-embracing humanism and true international outlook devoid of sectionalism and geographical differences. He aspires towards the type of education that existed in the heyday of Islam, that produced remarkable results. Briffault, the famous historian of civilisation, has summed it up like this – 'Science is the most momentous contribution of Arab civilisation to the modern world. Nowhere is this, i.e. the decisive influence of Islamic culture, so clear and momentous as in the genesis of that power which constitutes the distinctive force of the modern world and the supreme force of its victory – natural science and the scientific spirit'.

Even if the progress in scientific and technological fields in the Islamic states is at a low ebb after the early centuries of leading the world, yet overall education is thoroughly imbibed at the religious level. This has relevance for religious education in British Schools where a preponderance of Asians attend a primary school, (sometimes well over 50 per cent). There is a pressing need for religious education to cater for a multi-religious society. Even in the West, students are seeking beyond narrow religious boundaries and are looking outward to the good in all the world's faiths.

The biggest danger in excessive 'integration' is that children grow up not knowing about their own religion and history, thinking themselves 'English' but when they leave school disillusionment sets in and they are neither English nor Pakistani, neither Christian nor Muslim, rootless like the Negro youths in USA cities.

But theory is one thing, practice another. There are those Muslims who outwardly seem not to be practising the tenets of their faith, but who in the final analysis, would stand by their faith.

A drinking Muslim once had an argument with a non-Muslim who abused him and his religion. This is where those dealing with the issue and trying to bring reconcillation between the various elements of society will have to remember that a *non-practising Muslim* (one who drinks alchohol for instance) is unrepresentative of the integrity and true honour of the Muslim faith. Religious faith in a cross section of society is blind, for a very small proportion of the world's populace actually thinks out the beliefs handed down to it by its ancestors. Those who do ponder on such matters find them not at all easy to grasp. Islamic ideology has always laid great stress on reasoning out of natural phenomena, investigation of surroundings and harnessing of natural forces for human good.

Bibliography

Suggestions for further reading. Those books, published abroad can sometimes be ordered from Pakistani bookshops in Britain.

Islam, Alfred Guillaume; Penguin Book.

The Eternal Message of Mohammed, Abdul Rahman Aziz; A Mentor Book.

Introduction to Islam, Publication of Centre Cultural Islamique; Paris

The Saint of Jilan (*Ghaus-ul-Azam*), S. A. Salik; Ashraf Press, Lahore.

Anthology of Islamic Literature, James Kritzeck; Penguin Book.

The Darwishes or Oriental Spiritualism, J. P. Brown; Oxford, 1927.

The Spirit of Islam, Syed Amir Ali; University Paperback, Methuen, London.

Sufism – An Account of the Mystics of Islam, A. J. Arberry; George Allen and Unwin Ltd.

Muslim Institutions (Translation from the French by John P. Macgregor), Maurice Gaudefroy Demombynes; George Allen and Unwin Ltd.

Three Major Problems Confronting the World of Islam, Dr. Said Ramadan; Islamic Centre, Geneva.

Islam and Challenges of the Modern Times, A. K. M. Fazal-ul-Quadar Chaudary; The Motamar Al-Alam Al-Islami, Karachi.

The Meaning of the Glorious Quran, M. Pickthall; London, 1930.

Tafheem-ul-Quran (*Translation of the Holy Quran*), Maulana Abu-ala-Mahdood; Lahore.

A Manual of Hadith, M. Muhammed Ali; Lahore.

The Reconstruction of Religious Thought in Islam, Mohammed Iqbal; London.

Women in Islam, Mohammed Mazher-ud-Din Siddiqi, Lahore.

Islam in Theory and Practice, Maryam Jameelah (formerly Margaret Marcus), New York, Lahore.

Islam and Modernism, Maryam Jameelah; Lahore.

Iqbal, His Art and Thought, Syed Abdul Vahid; John Murray, London.

Kitab-ul-Amal-bil-Sunnate – Tarteeb Sharif (*The Holy Succession*), Barkat Ali, Salarwala (Lyallpur).

The Benefactor, Fakir Syed Waheed-ud-Din, Karachi.

SIKHISM
by
Peggy Holroyde

Historical background

Within the great land mass of India there are many major faiths which have
existed alongside each other – on the whole in harmony and tolerance. If ever
there was an example of a pluralistic society in which different religions and
races have somehow managed, despite certain historical disruptions, to create a
unified culture out of the diversity, the example is in this teeming sub-continent
of well over 540,000,000 people.

Not only are there 60,000,000 Muslims in present-day India (equivalent to a
third of the population of the Islamic state of Pakistan) but there are millions of
Buddhists, Jains, Christians of many persuasions, both indigenous Syrian
Christian tracing their ancestry from the conversion of six Brahmin families by
St Thomas of Antioch who landed on the Kerala coast in AD 52, or of later
conversion in the fifteenth century after the arrival of Vasco da Gama and the
Portuguese. In addition there are Black Jews and White Jews, and Parsees of
the Zoroastrian faith which spread from Persia in the eighth century.

There are also 7,000,000 Sikhs – most easily identifiable of all India's diverse
peoples by their strong physique, their mechanical knowhow, their beards and
their turbans. The Sikhs are not a different race of people; they are as Indian as
any other regional group, more than the Welsh are British, but they have been
moulded by their geographical, and therefore, historical experiences into a very
homogenous society with a strong and loyal sense of their own especial identity.

The Sikhs stood in the classic pathway of marauding invaders right from the
beginning of India's recorded history. These people were not then of this faith
but the Punjabi temperament had already been crystallised by the force of these
threatening experiences. They have had to respond in a united and concerted
fashion to defend the Punjab, the land of the five rivers – Punj, the Persian word
meaning 'five' and ab meaning 'water' or 'river' (Panch, the Hindu and Urdu
word for five has derived from this).

The alternative was decimation. Because of their toughness as a people the
Sikhs formed the strong arm of defence to the Indian Army in the days of the
British Raj. This they remember with some asperity when they face discrimina-
tion in this country; even the British Army did not enforce the tin helmet on to
their heads when they were fighting for a British cause in British battles but
allowed them the right to their turbans even in the first World War.

The effect of their being banded together for unity in defence of the gateway into the fertile plains of the Gangetic basin of North India has therefore made them fiercely resilient, individualistic, outgoing, always willing to work hard for themselves. They have been beholden to no one. This is why after the holocaust of Partition they have prided themselves on the remarkable recovery during total migration that overtook the Punjab, now divided between Pakistan and India. They also declare with conviction that they have hardly known a Sikh beggar in their midst.

Because of their history and geographical situation they have, like the Scots, migrated all over the world. In Canada there are now three to four generations of Sikhs in the Alberta and Vancouver regions who seem to have existed there without upheaval to the local community – but they have not lost their distinctive culture, and their daughters (even among the upper middle-classes), still effect arranged marriages with well-placed Sikh men back in the Punjab well over 9,000 miles away.

In Britain the Sikhs have continued this strong sense of community feeling and brotherhood, giving help to those who have newly arrived with little money and no home to go to. Their gurdwaras (house of the guru) are centres of welfare to give free food and shelter to these people until they find their own feet. Incidentally, this applies to anyone no matter what their religion is.

Obviously much of their strength has come from the nature of the Sikh faith, and the emphasis within it of brotherhood and service (sewa), which Guru Nanak, the founder of Sikhism in the 15th century, so unremittingly taught.

Sikhs maintain that their religion is an entirely organic growth, not an off-shoot of the main stem of Hinduism as was Buddhism or Jainism, both reform movements of two thousand years beforehand. Nevertheless, in the context of India, Sikhs are still deeply influenced by the surrounding culture of Hinduism, and their faith may be said to combine the essence of both Hindu and Muslim religious outlook at its best. In fact the mystic poetry of Guru Nanak is suffused with a mixture of Hindu and Muslim metaphysical thought, while at the same time declaring the irrelevancies of the outer forms and rituals of both.

The eminent historian, Arnold Toynbee, has written of the Sikhs in the UNESCO series on Comparative Religions:

'The Indian and Judaic religions are notoriously different in spirit, and where they have met, they have sometimes behaved like oil and vinegar. Their principal meeting ground has been India where Islam has impinged on Hinduism violently. On the whole the story of the relations between these two great religions has been an unhappy tale of mutual misunderstanding and hostility. Yet on both sides of this religious barrier there has been a minority of discerning spirits who have seen that, at bottom, Hinduism and Islam are each an expression of the same fundamental religious truth, and that these two expressions are therefore reconcilable with each other and are of supreme value when brought into harmony. The Sikh religion might be described, not inaccurately, as a vision of this Hindu-Muslim common ground. To have discovered and embraced the deep harmony underlying the historic Hindu-Muslim discord has been a noble spiritual triumph: and Sikhs may well be proud of their religion's ethics and origin.'

Certainly Guru Nanak, though born in a Hindu family of the Kshatriya caste (Brahmin, Kshatriya, Vaishya and Sudra being the four orders of caste) held many Muslim friends close to him and travelled all over the Muslim world – even to Mecca. But when he first took up his preaching he proclaimed: 'There is no Hindu, there is no Muslim'; and when he died both Hindus and Muslims claimed his body as their own.

The First Guru and how the Sikhs Emerged

Like so many other holy teachers, Guru Nanak, as a boy, had the same pull towards religious inquiry and meditation. In the true tradition of the saint he left his parents, his wife and his two sons, and took to the open road. As he moved around from village to village on foot (just as Christ had done, as Buddha had done, as Muhammed had done) he talked to the humble villagers and discoursed rather than preached. Holy men of India have done this time and again. Vinoba Bhave, Gandhi's chief disciple, is still doing this kind of padayatra, religious disciplinary pilgrimage on foot, to spread the word of God.

Guru Nanak's impact was heightened because of his own intensity of faith, and the historic moment in which this culminated.

The whole body of Hindu society and Hindu thought had been forced onto the defensive as a result of repeated waves of invasion from the 7th century onwards – from Huns and Arabs, and from the 11th century (at the same time as the Norman invasion of Britain), from Scythians and Parthians, Persians and Afghan Muslims.

These were mostly raiders who looted wealth, women and temple property. With the invasion of Emperor Babar in 1521, a different kind of Muslim rule occurred. The Moghuls were people who came to stay and settle in India, spreading their culture almost to the furthest reaches of the South where the most predominantly Hindu society existed untouched by grave social disruption.

The Moghuls effected a synthesis with the prevailing Hindu civilisation of the North and Central India, so creating a mixed Indian culture in which the two forces, sometimes hostile, sometimes harnessed in harmony, came together under such magnanimous spirits as the great Emperor Akbar (an exact contemporary of Elizabeth 1) who took a Hindu wife and encouraged Jesuits and Buddhists, Hindus and English Protestants to visit his court and debate in free religious atmosphere the great spiritual truths. From this forging of the two strains the secular state of India as we know her today, has grown.

The progress, however, of this development was never even. At stages when Hinduism was precariously situated under more iconoclastic Moghul Emperors such as Aurengzeb and was further pushed on to the defensive by the advent of European traders and their accompanying wars and converting missionaries, there was no impetus towards change in the Hindu body politic. Society became ingrown and rigidly restricted by caste to hold the people together under all these alien influences. Ritual was essential to maintain the status quo of the temple religion. Both Hindu and Muslim women went into purdah as a defence mechanism, although the zenana quarters allocated for women in the rear of the houses, and the wearing of the tent-like burqah, were never prevalent in the original Hindu society of the Vedas or the Epics, nor in Buddha's time. Muhammed himself was quite uncompromisingly recorded on how women should be protected and equally treated legally, emotionally and economically. In the Quran it is written: '. . . your women, they are a garment unto you, and ye are a garment unto them'. Arabic society however neglected this injunction.

In India the strength of peasant society was held steadfast in rigid custom and submission to the rulings of caste and temple priest. There was little room for new ideas or the creative impulses of artistic expression during the ten centuries of invasion and foreign rule with their attendant conversions to Muslim and Christian faiths.

It is against this background that the impassioned insight of Guru Nanak flourished. Even in his childhood he was precocious; he preferred the company of wandering holy men; he had always been of a meditative disposition.

One story is told of him that at the age of nine he was perspicacious enough to refuse to wear the sacred thread Hindus of high caste tie around their chests at their 'naming' ceremonies when a boy becomes of sufficient age to understand the main tenets of his faith. Nanak is said to have announced to the family priest that such a cotton thread, triply twisted as symbolic of the three kinds of knowledge, no matter how supposedly sacred, had not prevented men from acting in an evil way; he went on to declare that the only meaningful 'sacred thread' for mankind was to turn heart and mind towards meditation upon the name of the ONE GOD – and one could not love God without first learning to love each other.

But perhaps the most famous story told of Nanak is that of his falling asleep with his feet towards the Kaaba in Mecca, an unpardonable insult to Allah. The outraged Muslim Imam woke him up and reprimanded him. Nanak's reply is typical – 'If you think I do wrong by pointing my feet towards the house of God, then turn them in some other direction where God does not dwell'.

Discipleship and the Gurus

In the last fifteen years of his life, Guru Nanak settled down to preach the truth in uncompromisingly monotheistic terms about the Oneness of God. The shishyus (Sanskrit word for disciples) who gathered around him gave the name in a Punjabi form – Sikh – to the newly emerging restatement of belief in an indivisiable God.

The shishyu became the Sikh.

The role of the Guru became very important in the Sikh religion.

'As is God, so is the Guru; and as is the Guru, so must be the follower.'

The more one explores the spiritual content of the Sikh belief, the more one is aware of the potency of this recognition of the power of the Guru. He is not so much a person in the shape of a living Guru so much as a transcendental creative force coming down through the ages to reside in each individual believer, a touchstone for the union of individual with God.

But also at the wider level all ten of the Sikh Gurus or teachers welded a whole people into a 'continuous course of training' as a Sikh commentator has said, 'in wisdom and experience spread over many generations before they could be sure that the people so trained had acquired a character of their own'.

Love of the Name

In the Japji of morning prayer of meditation which all Sikhs recite in their devotional gatherings, Guru Nanak declared:

> 'There is One God,
> Eternal Truth is His Name:
> Maker of all things
> Fearing nothing, and at enmity with nothing.
> Timeless in His Image;
> Not begotten, being of His own Being
> By the grace of the Guru, made known to men.
> True in the beginning, true throughout the ages.'

God is described as nirgun (Sanskrit: without material quality or image) and sagun (with form). The Sikh view combines both the Aryan concept of the immanence of God (existing in all things) – that He is in us and we are in God (Tat Twam Asi) with the Semitic idea of transcendence – that He is beyond human existence and the creation of the world and would exist even if mind was not there to conceive of His existence.

When God made Himself manifest to us, related in a personal way, to humanity he became what is called The Name: Ek Omkar – There is One God.

The Japji says in the twenty-first verse:

> 'Pilgrimages, penances, compassion and almsgiving
> Bring a little merit, the size of a sesame seed,
> But he who learns, and believes and loves The Name
> Shall bathe and be made clean
> In a place of pilgrimage within him'.

and again

> 'All creation is His Word made manifest'.

There are overtones here of the Gospel words of Christianity:
> 'In the beginning was the Word; and the Word was made God'.

It is this idea of God within each man and woman that suffuses all of Guru Nanak's teaching and that of the following nine Gurus.

Guru Tegh Bahadur, father of the last Guru Gobind Singh, who lived in the 17th century, wrote this:

'He lives in all, is yet ever distinct: He abides within thee too.
As fragrance dwells in a flower, or reflection in a mirror'.

The revelation of God is to be found in the sacred word – Ek Omkar, the Name of God. The repetitive recalling of the Creator's Name (known as Simran) by the chanting of 'Waheguru' is the outstanding characteristic of the Sikh faith which is simple and straightforward and shorn of abtruse philosophy and its attendant metaphysics. One could liken the Sikh attitude to worship to those in the Hindu tradition who follow Bhakti – the path of loving devotion towards a God who cares for his human creation in immediate and personal terms, or the Quakers in Christian tradition.

Within this direct and uncomplicated view of Godhead, Sikhism came to react against the extreme attitudes held by some Hindus that all creation was Maya or illusion. To Sikhs the universe is

1. Very real because God's presence is *within* it.
2. His presence is not disinterested in the sense of a detached scientific concept of an Impersonal Neuter, Brahm, beyond and outside of this planet's existence and humanity's personal concerns.
3. God is a presence here upon earth, in the sense of intelligence.
4. He is indivisibly One without division of Trinity either in the Hindu or Christian tradition.
5. He has indelibly imprinted His Name in all men by means of a moral presence.
6. There is no idea of a monopoly of Truth for any one people, race or creed in that God being indivisible belongs to all people, no matter how they (with limited human vision) have cared to conceive Him.
7. The only way to realisation of Him and the fulfilment of individual personality in Him is through love and faith.
8. The only way to worship Him is to sing His praises and to meditate upon His Name.

The repeating of the Holy Name is not a mere mechanical device just as the 'telling' of a rosary for a Catholic should not be. As in both, the essence of the religious exercise is so to train the mind that it recalls the qualities and aspects of God and infuses them into the personality of the worshipper. This after all is what religious disciplines should be about – to lift us out of the narrow world of our self-centredness up to another plane where the vision of God makes us think beyond ourselves.

This 'knowledge' of God arouses wismad or wonder in the believer, which is expressed in the Sikh expression of greeting: 'Waheguru . . . The wonderful Lord'.

Karma and Grace

Guru Nanak, although living in a predominantly Hindu society where the theory of karma and reincarnation was prevalent, taught that this law, while accepting the truth that right action attains salvation, is not immutable. People are not condemned to a certain state of life and a lowly position in society as a result of past actions in a previous incarnation. Instead he preached the belief that Grace (similar to the Christian viewpoint) can intervene, and if a man truly surrenders himself to God, in the sense of forgetfulness of self, he can so transform his personality that he frees himself from the rigidity of Karma.

Caste and the Brotherhood of Men

Consequent upon this belief, the Sikh followers of the first Guru were able to escape the stranglehold of caste rigidity. Caste as an idea had come into Hinduism during the period when priests had become over important. There are always historical trends this way in all religions. In India during the 15th and 16th centuries hierarchical tendencies were implacably to the fore in Hindu social life because of the menace from without.

In Nanak's teaching, that a man could be blessed by his devotion to the Name of God, and therefore to His Spirit, the possibilities of individual freedom were immense. There was a profound sense of release for the Sikh believer.

'Recognise all human nature as one', declared the tenth Guru, Gobind Singh, '. . . All have the same eyes, the same ears, the same body and the same build – a compound of the same five elements', panch tãt as the Sikh calls them in prayer.

This egalitarian view of the essential unity and equality of mankind found tangible form under the guidance of Guru Gobind Singh. He was to prove in one dramatic gesture that a man was not to be honoured for his position in society through caste, or for his monopoly of truth through a spiritual creed, but for what he held in his heart and his mind as an emanation of God who resided in him.

This fundamental belief in the inner God within each person has marked out the social organisation and character of the Sikhs to a very noticeable degree so that although they, like any other group of human beings, stratify themselves into certain class structures, they do have much more mobility within their society and are on the whole extremely loyal to each other, and help each other out in the difficult circumstances of migration.

Sangat or Organisation

The idea of the brotherhood of mankind was buttressed by (a) the organisation that Guru Gobind Singh brought into being in the 17th century, and (b) the quality of service (or sewa) to the community at large which has been fostered by the clear-cut nature of this organisation or sangat. There has always been emphatic teaching by all the Gurus on the importance of work well done in this very real world.

Sikhs are in the main not prone to asceticism or the contemplative life. They are the activists of India. Theirs is not a belief in 'cloister'd virtue', cut off from involvement with fellow men either in the Christian monastic system or in the Hindu meditative withdrawal, into cave or ashram. A Sikh must test himself in the outside world, amid the temptations of life. Only then can he fire himself in the crucible of experience and emerge as – a most fitting word for Sikhs in general – a 'robust' person.

The Khalsa

In 1699 the last Guru knit the whole society of Punjabi Sikhs together into a homogeneous and identifiable religious community by forming what is called 'the Khalsa' – a word meaning pure.

This event is celebrated annually at the Sikh Spring Festival of Baisakhi, the beginning of the Sikh New Year, which is now commemorated on 13 April.

During the 17th century the Sikhs were under constant persecution from both Muslim rulers and Hindu Rajas who resented their defiance of long-established codes of conduct and caste ritual. Guru Gobind Singh, a deeply religious and learned man, felt that the warriors of the Punjab needed to be able to defend themselves in these ever-present skirmishes. He summoned a great gathering of his people on the Baisakhi Day, which has become the most important day of the Sikh year. This meeting had been widely publicised not only in the Punjab; it involved people from widely different regions and backgrounds. At this gathering he appeared on a platform before them with his sword and appealed for one among their number to come forward and offer his head for the faith and the cause of righteousness, not only of the Sikhs but of *all* the communities affected by the turmoil of the times.

There was consternation. No one answered. He repeated his plea once more, and then a third time. It was at this point that one in the multitude took his life in his hands and acquiesced to the Guru's demand for sacrifice. Five Sikhs, one after the other, disappeared behind the public platform with only Guru Gobind Singh appearing again with his sword dripping with what seemed like blood.

Then he dumbfounded the gathering by bringing out all five men – unharmed and intact. He took these five as his beloved five followers – Panch Pyaras (Five Beloved).

The five redoubtable warriors, one a Jat (landed gentry), one a Kshatriya, and three of low caste origin, who had offered their lives to prove their loyalty to the cause of the Sikhs, were then baptised by him. This baptism consisted – and still consists within Sikh ceremonies – of the sprinkling of the holy water or nectar– Amrit which is made from water and a special sugar stirred by a double-sided sword in an iron vessel – over the freshly-washed hair and eyes of the follower of Sikh belief. For this baptism ceremony nowadays, people must be properly bathed beforehand and clad in clean attire.

After this ceremony the Panch Pyaras drank a little of the Amrit altogether as a declaration of their equality one with another, saying after the Guru:

'Waheguruji ka Khalsa . . . Waheguruji ka Fateh (Hail God of the Pure, Hail God of Victory)' – the suffix Ji being a mark of affectionate respect added on to names by Indians when they speak of such evocative teachers and leaders as Gandhiji and Panditji (Nehru).

These five were then given the Five symbols of Five K's which set the Sikhs apart as a religious group. These are:

1. **keshas**
    Uncut hair which has always been a symbol throughout all civilisations of

saintliness – Christ Himself is always depicted with long flowing hair, and Buddha's was tied up in a top-knot. Thus uncut hair eventually called for a covering to keep it in order and so the turban evolved.

2. kanga

The comb to keep the hair tidy by tying it in a bun on top of the head. The turban has become the most identifiable object to stand as a symbol of the passions and prejudices aroused on all sides when matters of integration, cultural diversity and questions of conformity within a native community arise. Many a Sikh can be asked why the use of the turban arose. A good many will not know the answer beyond the fact that it is part of a Sikh's outward religious adherence to the Sikh faith. The fact that quite a few Sikhs have shaved their beards and cut their hair serves to confuse many British people even more so about the sanctity of the turban. Not only does this happen in this country to make it easier to get employment, but also back in India as part of modern urban living where it is difficult to wash and dry the hair as quickly or as easily as one can by sitting or walking in a village under the burning sun in an atmosphere of acceptance of these age old customs. But in all religions there are non-conformists.

The Turban

The fact is that the turban cannot be equated with other forms of headgear. It is not as the fez is to the Turk, or the stetson to the Texan or even the bowler hat to the British. The British Army bowed its unyielding regulations to the force of Sikh feeling on the turban so that in the trenches in the first world war the Sikh was not forced to remove his turban for the tin helmet and he died and won his V.Cs in the defence of British policies with his turban on his head.

Many a Sikh will say that the turban arose out of the need to keep the long uncut hair tidy, and for convenience's sake. Certainly in India the use of wrapped cotton lengths on the head for the farmer working under the implacable Indian sun became a necessity to keep the head protected. But there are other reasons which go deeper into the religious origins of the Sikh community.

The institution of the turban is secular in its origin, if we go back further than Punjab.

Originally it was the Muslim invaders from the Middle East who introduced the turban into Punjab. The extreme heat necessitated the covering of head in the regions of Middle East and Arabia.

The first people ever to wear turbans were the Emperors of the Slave Dynasty beginning with King Subuktgeen.

There is no mention of a turban in Hindu lore. The Gods and mythological heroes are depicted wearing long hair, with or without beard (beards are generally worn by the sages). The headdress is generally golden mukats (crowns) with inlaid jewels, but never, never turbans.

Even Rajputs wore turbans, but *after* and not *before* the Muslim invaders came on the scene.

The above is a purely secular explanation of the institution of the turban. The religious necessity is obvious since the wearing of long hair and its proper upkeep is obligatory, which a Sikh will not find easy to relinquish.

Until say, 25 years ago, the wearing of a turban was an important attribute of a 'gentleman' be he Hindu, Muslim or a Sikh. 'Pagg-Bannh' was a term indicating a respectable individual, paggri being the Indian word for turban. Guru Gobind Singh made it obligatory for Sikhs to wear the turban. Out of the saintliness of his nature he wished to save innocent bystanders from being picked out for beheading during a period when militant Sikh armies were suffering torture by this method during the invasions of the Punjab by the Muslims. If a Sikh suffered for his faith that was right and proper but if others were mistaken for Sikhs and suffered, that was morally wrong. So he perpetuated the turban as a distinctive feature so outwardly recognisable that no Sikh could be mistaken for an adherent of any other religion than he was.

Throughout Asia the wearing of headgear is a mark of respect – turbans are exchanged between Sikh and Sikh, and Sikh and non-Sikh as a token of deep friendship. Often this leads to the opposite of our own custom in Britain where headgear is removed indoors. In Asia it is the reverse – headgear is kept *on* inside a temple, mosque or gurdwara. This custom has been carried to this country and it is nothing strange to see even a Western cloth hat or trilby worn by some Asians to committee meetings or general assemblies. Westerners should also wear headgear if attending a service or a wedding in a Sikh gurdwara.

3. kirpan

The short two-edged sword for defence, is also a symbol of dignity. Guru Gobind Singh said: 'When affairs are past other remedies, it is justifiable to unsheath the sword'.

The shorter version of a sword, the size of a dagger is also included. The double-edged sword, is Khanda, which is concavely curved on the sides, and sharpened both sides. Khanda – meaning 'disintegrator'.

4. kara

The steel bangle worn on the right wrist by all Sikhs, men and women, as a symbol of the philosophical concept of unity of God being concentric – having no beginning and no end, and a reminder that Sikhs should not commit any misdeed by the use of the hand. (This is therefore not a piece of jewellery. Some teachers might mistake it in school and demand its removal.)

The bangle is a constant reminder to a Sikh that he is a 'prisoner' of the values of life he professes as a Sikh, and since an average human uses his right hand mostly, it is worn on the right wrist, as a perpetual reminder of a Sikh's obligations.

5. **kachcha**

A pair of short under-pants to enable brisk movement in comparison with the unserviceability of the flowing dhoti or pyjama trousers commonly worn by Indians – especially for the warrior saints whom Sikhs were to become. Also the kachcha was to remind them of sexual discipline.

After these symbols were initiated at this first Baisakhi ceremony, each believer took the name of Singh and Kaur for men and women respectively, renounced former caste, and swore to be brothers one with another.

Guru Gobind Singh further astonished the large audience by then asking his new disciples to baptise him in turn, in somewhat like fashion as Christ asked John the Baptist. In the light of a Guru's elevated position in the Indian mind this was remarkable but served the purpose of instilling in the Sikh mind that ultimate authority resided not in the Guru, who is still human and not a divine revelation, but in the One God. One Sikh commentator, Teja Singh, has written in his book on Sikhism that it was also important to show that the Guru, although sinless, was not above man's capacity to imitate if he was to be effective as a Guru, a condition difficult to fulfil if he were a supernatural being.

Guru Gobind Singh became a member of the new Khalsa brotherhood and before he died he dismantled the tradition of human Gurus by preaching that the Adi Granth, the collection of mystic poems, hymns and other sayings of the Ten Gurus, was now to be regarded as the final Guru for all time. This is why the Holy Book or Granth Sahib as it is sometimes called is treated with such reverence and bedecked with orange marigolds (so often used in many Indian sacred ceremonies) and carried on a decorated float when taken out in procession in Indian Sikh ceremonies.

It was at this point in time that the Khalsa were forbidden to smoke tobacco, cut their hair, drink alcohol or take drugs such as hemp or bhang which were smoked in the rural communities, or eat meat slaughtered in the Muslim fashion.

Adi Granth or Granth Sahib, The Sikh Scripture

The Holy Book of the Sikhs (Adi = the FIRST) is now regarded as the living progressive voice, both in time and concept, of all the ten Gurus. It comprises their teachings, prayers and songs of praise, plus those of some Hindu and Muslim saints, because they contained no dogmatic creed or absolute doctrine and were applicable to all ages, and flexible because they acknowledged the absolute truths of Love and Service. Only through Love for the Name of God and through realising that God is only attainable through service done within the world and for fellow men, is a man's fulfilment achieved.

This Holy Book is called the Adi Granth to distinguish it from the Works of Guru Gobind Singh – known as the Dasam Granth.

Sri Guru Granth Sahib is *not* a collection of mystic poems. If a gross over-simplification can be forgiven it could be said that it is a very detailed logical discussion of all the available religious thought and the eventual distillation of all thought content effected in an intelligent, logical, manner, Semitic and anti-Semitic included.

When the Sikhs pay homage to the Guru Granth Sahib, it is not the bookform that is being worshipped, but the Spirit of Guru Nanak, in all its ten subsequent forms, expressed in the form of Poetry, and the writing and spirit of other contributors whose writings had been accepted by the Gurus, as being eligible, to be included in it.

In it is reflected not only the philosophical teachings of Nanak but the living out in practical human terms which Nanak achieved in his life of devotion and love for God. The songs of the Adi Granth are to be sung – but they are redolent of a very deep belief in the brotherhood of Man, restraint of passions, a search for the fulfilment of self, and service – service emphatically underlined by all the Gurus after Nanak.

Also the Adi Granth is essentially practical – it encourages a man to live a normal properly fulfilled life in this world – to enjoy sex, prosperity, the complete family life, always within the framework though of acknowledging these blessings as being gifts from the love of God for mankind. There is no taint of 'original sin'; this applies to Hinduism also.

In this sense, in the practicalities of religion, the Sikhs have their feet very much on the ground.

'He alone treadeth the path of righteousness', sayeth Nanak, 'who earneth his bread with honest labour and shareth it with others'.

This is fundamental to an understanding of the Sikhs. Partly because of their protein-filled diet in one of the most progressive agricultural regions of India the Sikhs are activists in this world. They do work hard – but this is emphasised again and again in their religious book. Earning one's bread by worthwhile labour, sharing these earnings with the needy and meditating on the holy name of The Lord Divine is a convenient summing up of the fundamental teachings of Sikhism.

The Adi Granth is always revered and placed in a central position for congregational worship in a Sikh temple, called Gurdwara (Darwaza meaning door or gateway, implying therefore that the Gurdwara is the gateway to the Guru). Sikhs bow down to it as the Guru and always sit lower than the Adi Granth itself. This is why the tradition has arisen of sitting cross-legged on the floor without chairs or cushions to show that despite wealth or position or background each Sikh is one with another, equal in the sight of One God.

The Sikh Religious Service

Homage is paid to the Shabd or Word; this is the reason why the Granth is always kept in a clean cloth, is opened under a canopy and a fly-whisk or silver-handled chowri is kept near at hand to wave over it, this being a traditional Indian symbol of those in authority.

The usual order of service for a Sikh congregation is the Opening of the Book, bhajans or hymns of the various Gurus set to certain ragas or musical modes, the sermon which can be given by any member – there being no order of priests – the Anand or prayer of thanksgiving, and a further reading from the Guru Granth Sahib.

After this the Karah Prasad (a token of God's benevolence) is distributed and eaten. This is similar in concept to communion food, but consists of semolina, milk, a little clarified butter and sugar boiled together, cooked by individual Sikh families and stirred with the kirpan, and brought to the Gurdwara for all to eat as a symbol of the social equality of each worshipper at the conclusion of the service. Nanak had instituted this ceremony as part of his religious defiance of caste restrictions on intercaste eating and the idea of untouchability which had so damaged later Hindu social structure.

The Position of Women

It is very noticeable in Britain that Sikh women are more often in evidence and more outgoing, both in meeting the British and in dealing with family affairs, say in relation to teachers, than many of their Asian sisters. This has its reasons in the emphatic teaching of social equality from all the Gurus, not only in the sense of equality that is created by the positive idea of brotherhood amongst all Sikhs but also in the inevitable corollary that women too should be treated as equals.

Because of the nature of the turbulent history of the Punjab and the necessity for the Sikhs to band together for their self-defence, women played a strong and assertive role in their families. Even in the purely religious sense they have always been allowed to participate in and conduct ceremonies in the Gurdwara.

'How can they be regarded as inferior', Guru Nanak exclaimed, 'when they give birth to the greatest men'.

His reasoning was that if God is immanent, present in a divine, creative form within each human being, women as well as men share in the Grace of God and are as equal in the eyes of God, both in spirit and in responsibility.

'Women are the conscience of men', another Guru wrote.

Although Sikh women do take the plunge more readily into British society and are willing to eat and converse with British people, they are still extremely modest and home-loving by Western standards and tend still in mixed company to separate in a room, gathering in a corner among other women. But this custom is common all over Asia and only among the most sophisticated and educated people do women accept the custom of Western mixing of the sexes in social get-togethers, and even then the great majority retain a very welcome modesty and gentle feminity.

Social Customs

Greetings

The most common form of Sikh greeting among themselves and for Westerners going into their homes is to place the palms together at chest level like the Hindu 'Namasteh' greeting and say, 'Sat Sri Akal', which means God is Truth. At larger gatherings the cry is made, 'Waheh Guruji Ka Khalsa' – which means the Khalsa are the chosen of God, to which the reply comes 'Waheh Guruji Ki Fateh' – God be victorious.

Fasting and Clothes

The Sikh scripture does not say fasting is essential as a religious austerity, but can be undertaken for health reasons and for personal discipline.

Again there are no restrictions on what a Sikh eats or wears. On the whole Sikhs take a liberal view in these matters and are easily adaptable to their new surroundings. They are a meat-eating people on the whole: there are few vegetarian Sikhs and clothing is only regarded as suspect if it is provocative to the passions – again the mini-skirt comes in for comment. However, modern Punjabi girls have also taken to tight-fitting mini-Kameez!

Eating habits

There is some consternation in schools and hospitals when Asian children and adults are discovered eating with their fingers. This is a universal social custom in Asia and is NOT born out of poverty or backwardness. The logic of thinking is perfectly valid. Fingers are as sensible an instrument for the eating of food and a good deal cleaner than some cutlery wiped dry with a dirty dish towel. Almost without exception Indians and Pakistanis from force of habit as well as religious custom, wash their hands before meals, and afterwards. To them, therefore, it is reasonable to assume that the hand is more free from germs than a knife and fork they have not seen washed. Besides fingers are more convenient for eating Asian type food.

Many Westerners, especially children, find a new adventure and freedom, when in Asia in eating this way off beautifully polished pewter talas or flat dishes, or even freshly plucked banana leaves. There is very great delight in eating, sitting cross-legged on a rush mat, on the ground, with a mound of white rice against such a green background, surrounded also by scrupulously clean bowls of varied spiced delicacies to be added, by hand, and put in the mouth deftly. Eating in such circumstances becomes a serious matter – and an adventure.

Naming – Forename

The christening ceremony of a baby is simple. The Guru Granth is opened at random and the first letter of the first word on the uppermost paragraph of the left hand page is the beginning letter for the forename of the child – this corresponds to our Christian name.

Naming – Surname

British people in contact with Sikhs sometimes get confused over the surname and mistake the name Singh given to all male Sikhs and Kaur to females (married and single) as the surname. This is not so.

Singh is part of the forename and in actual fact the surname is the sub-caste name borne by a whole family, or the village name – such as Kairon. (Sikhs disassociated themselves from caste but in the Indian context these names, such as Sondh, Gill, Dhesi, Sambhi, Sandhu, have crept back recently to common usage). To add further confusion, however, these sub-caste names are dropped and a man who started off with a first name Piara, then the distinctive Singh, then his sub-caste name Sambhi – Piara Singh Sambhi – may eventually be known as Mr Piara Singh.

Sometimes other names derived from trade guilds or confederations which grew up after the disintegration of the Moghul Empire – Ramgarhia for instance – are used as surnames.

Marriages
Marriages are:
1. Monogamous.
2. A second marriage is only allowed if there is no issue from the first.
3. If a brother dies it has been the custom for the wife to be adopted by the remaining brother to give her some social status and to save her from the very real perils and loneliness of widowhood which was the fate of Hindu women.
4. Nanak forbade the infanticide of girl babies and 'sati' and reinstated the power and dignity of the woman which had been originally honoured in Hinduism but had undergone humiliation due to centuries of invasion.
5. Attitudes to modern methods of family-planning are very straightforward, and favourable.

The wedding ceremony is much simpler than for the Hindu and takes place below the Adi Granth. A white cloth is laid on the floor and guests bow low and place money on this as they enter. Men usually sit one side of the hall, women on the other, and heads must be covered. There is no fire to be walked around as in a Hindu wedding.

Death
Death is regarded as the gateway to salvation. Bodies are cremated perfectly normally at a crematorium after relatives have paid respects and read Sikh hymns over the dead body in their home. Kirtans or hymns are also chanted at a simple ceremony in the crematorium.

Conclusion
'The way of religion, as shown by Sikhism, is not a set of views or doctrines, but a way of life lived according to a definite model. It is based, not on rules or laws but upon discipleship. The personality of the Guru is at all times operative in the career of the disciple, commanding his whole being and shaping his life to its diviner issues'. So writes Teja Singh in *Sikhism: Its Ideals and Institutions*.

The teachings of the Gurus certainly do not dogmatise, nor do they seek to convert. The Sikh faith is in this respect the least proselytising of religions. In fact the concluding sentence in the Sikh temple prayers includes people of every faith. There is no creed, no legalistic injunctions on how to order society, no Ten Commandments. Their lives are moved more by a few fundamental, ethical motives which are basic to all the major faiths of this planet. Allied to these principles of behaviour, is a passionate love of God for His own sake and because the very beauty of His perfection inspires a human being in search of Him, to love him spontaneously; and secondly that this love, once experienced, impels a man or woman to express it to fellow human beings through service towards them.

All human life is a rediscovering of that inner perfection, God's creative gift to man, which we have lost because of the counter existence of the evil forces also at work within this world and in the minds of men.

Bibliography

The Sikhs, Khushwant Singh; Allen & Unwin, 1953.

The Sikhs Today, Khushwant Singh; Orient Longmans, New Delhi.

The Sacred Writings of the Sikhs, Allen & Unwin, 1960. (translation under the auspices of the National Academy of Letters, India).

An Introduction to Sikh Belief, Guru Gobind Singh, A Brief Outline of the Sikh Faith, Mrs P. M. Wylam; The Sikh Cultural Society, 88 Mollison Way, Edgware, Middlesex.

Guru Gobind Singh, Harbans Singh; Guru Gobind Singh Foundation, 50 MLA's Flats, Chandigarth. Reprinted by Tricentenary Committee, 38 Gloucester Circus, London SE10.

The Sikh Courier, Journal of The Sikh Cultural Society, 88 Mollison Way, Edgware, London.

Sikhism: Its Ideals and Institutions, Teja Singh; Orient Longmans Ltd, 1938.

A Critical Study of Adi-Granth, Dr Surinder Singh.

The Temple of Bread and the Sikh Guru, Pakarsh Singh.

The Quintessence of Sikhism, Professor Gobind Singh Mansukhani; Shromani Gurdwara. Parbandhak Mansukhani Committee, Amritsar.

Philosophy of Sikhism, Dr Sher Singh; Sterling Publishers Ltd, Delhi, 6.

Outlines of Sikh Thought, Dr Surinder Singh Kohli; Punjabi Prakashak Devnagar Karolbagh, N. Delhi, 5.

Transformation of Sikhism, Sir Gokul Chand Narang; New Book Society of India, New Delhi.

CUSTOMS

Social Customs more Asian than specifically Religious

Many social customs and attitudes in Asia have through the long process of time been given the final sanction of religious tradition – but in reality they have no reference in religious scripture, nor compulsion in moral law. They have been arrived at by the process of experience and experiment for almost twice as long as the European attempts at civilisation. This is the reason why they carry with them a subtle sense of racial superiority and why also Asians feel deep down in their hearts that the West has much to answer for.

There is an old story among the Nagas, the headhunting tribe of N.E. India, that God tried hard to make man in his own image. First he put him in the oven to cook, and burnt him. Thus the black races were created. Then God tried again and under-cooked him – this was the white race. The third time he tried – successfully this time – for man came out of the oven a nice golden brown!

Many Asians coming to the West have had a golden dream of European civilisation, imbibed from years of rule from British, French, Dutch and Portugese; from Christian schooling; from close contact with our university world, and the culture of our literature.

Living with us in the raw is a great cultural shock for them also. They see the seamy side of our lives as well: perhaps the *greatest* single shock to their systems after the colour question (and *their* own sense of superiority here) is the way we treat our elderly people. Again and again this comes up in conversation.

Joint Family

Such an attitude arises from the gigantic strength and enclosure of their extended family system where joint households of three or four generations still live under one roof. Although this is very gradually being eroded among the educated classes by urbanisation, and the individual nuclear family such as our own which is becoming the pattern of much urban life, still over 80 per cent of the people of India and Pakistan live in the villages – and this is where the population explosion is occurring so extremely. It will take, therefore, generations yet to change this vast area of society. And even those who have moved out of its sphere of activity still feel its influence and retain one foot in the village. There are families comprising more than 100 members living together under one roof. No child therefore ever feels neglected – even in the poorest families – and the duties and burdens of family life are shared. The isolation of Western urban life can therefore be a very great psychological shock to Asian women used to a wide-ranging network of family relationships.

The first thing an outsider notices in Asia is the very moving respect for elders of the family and a welcome affectionate respect for the parents. The second is the confusing and almost unlearnable names with which each relative is designated – a different word in Urdu and Hindi is given to the grandparents on the paternal side from those on the maternal side. Nana is the maternal grandfather, Baba is the paternal grandfather. An uncle older than the father has a different name from the younger brother of a child's father. So it goes on. In Bengali there are 64 different words for various relatives!

The joint family is built up on this great cohesive sense of unity. In a continent without national insurance or a welfare state, the extended family is one great insurance policy. The eldest son carries a heavy burden of financial responsibility when the parents can no longer labour in the fields or factories. It is a moral obligation to support the old people. This is carried over in this country so that old people make far less drain on our welfare services than our own old age pensioners do where their own younger members have deserted them. Even individual villages take responsibility for distant kin, and unearning members such as unmarried women can become an unbearable burden on the earning members of a family. This can lead to confusions for immigration officers and officials in Britain. Sometimes Asian children can quite genuinely look on a relative as a 'father', who has their total welfare in hand. This is an accepted custom in Asia, and explains why teachers who wish to see a child's parents may be visited by a distant relative instead.

Asian relatives come to stay – and stay for months. Asians accept this and the crowding and the consequent personal inconvenience without demur.

Family property is often pooled and daughters-in-law bring their dowry wealth into the joint family. Nowadays dowries are forbidden by Indian law (the Hindu Code Bill of the 1950s). Law may legislate but social custom dies hard, and still a good deal of hard bargaining can go on before a marriage is arranged.

Hospitality. Another shock to both Pakistanis and Indians is the diminished sense of hospitality in the West. They may not even realise that among British people themselves relationships are more formal and reticent, that we do not easily drop in on each other unannounced (nor at all times of night!), whereas they extend a very warm welcome to the stranger however unexpected he may be. Atithi – the Sanskrit word for guest – the stranger who comes unannounced, 'undated' is the literal meaning – is regarded as the honoured guest. This is why when any Westerner visits an Asian household they continue their overwhelming hospitality even to the point of overloading a plate with food so that it makes it very difficult either to eat it all up – or to refuse! Even on Christian festivals in India or Pakistan, Asians return the compliment by bringing gifts as well as on their own festivals.

Within the family the attitudes of Indians to *marriage and divorce* are very little different to those of Pakistanis. The arranged marriage is almost universal with perhaps nowadays a 'vetting' of each other by the young couple and a chance to withdraw if they cannot stand the sight of each other. Otherwise such marriages within their own environment and culture have proved as equally successful as the Western opposite approach. 'You fall in love, marry and repent at leisure' – says the Asian. 'We marry and then fall in love. Then there is less chance of disillusion.' Problems arise however in this country where children, especially girls, have grown up with one foot in our culture, and imbibed western ideas of personal freedom and permissiveness through primary and secondary school education. Cases of rebellion and deep tension are growing. A custom that is valid in an environment where it is universally practiced, is very hard to enforce where other girls, the majority, are clearly seen to live entirely differently, and many uneducated Asian parents do not fully make allowance for the overwhelming pressures on their teenagers.

At the Indian village level caste and subcaste or gotras still influence the choice of partner but at the educated level even Muslim and Hindu are marrying each other occasionally. *Divorce* is very rare – the only ground is adultery, or infertility on the part of either partner, in which case a second marriage is allowed. However, if the reason for divorce is inabililty to produce children the first wife must be maintained properly and supported by the husband as a member of the family. Muslim, Hindu and Sikh societies all have a system whereby elders of the family and the village use their good offices to try and bring about reconciliation or to smooth out tensions. Because of the nature of immigration and the resultant break-up of families this force for good is sadly lacking in Britain.

In modern urban families back in Asia greater freedom of choice is being given to sons and daughters to seek out their partners for life – but always under the close guidance of the parents. This is on the whole accepted. There are some young people who rebel but it is their marriages that are more likely to founder as they run against very strong currents in society and the binding agents of interwoven family life.

The position of women causes some ambivalence of attitude. The results of social customs grown out of historical developments where women had to be protected against abduction, clash with the philosophical idea of complete equality.

However at the city level educated women have in some instances more freedom than in the West in that domestic help is much more easily obtained and they can call on the help of many relatives also if they wish to run careers as well as homes.

Strangely enough at village level where women are labourers in the fields, in road-making, in building hydro-electric schemes and dams, they also can be fairly militant and free within a given framework. Throughout the sub-continent there is a universal respect for women, especially the mother, who enjoys a status within the home to be envied by her Western sisters. For a foreign woman too, Asia is perhaps one of the safest areas in the world in which to travel alone. In South India there is a long established matriachal system of society where all money is passed down through the female side of the family. Here women had a long tradition of education. There have been women philosophers, warrior leaders, politicians and saints who have given the lie to the image of the retiring Asian woman totally subjected to male rule. There is no doubt that due to man-made customs Asian women have suffered the same disability as Western women socially and economically. Purdah is still in existence in remote areas and in some less-well educated homes. But because an Asian woman is by nature more modest and retiring it does not necessarily mean to say that she has an inferior position *within* the family structure. Her *actual* status as a mother is unquestionable and her children pay her far more attention and respect than a good many Western mothers receive.

There is an Urdu saying: 'If you are seeking heaven look for it under your mother's feet'.

Because very educated Asian women are as emancipated and are holding responsible jobs in business and Government as in the West (sometimes ironically more so) does not mean to say that they behave socially in quite the same manner as Western women. Long tradition, and even a desire to remain very modest and graceful, influences their outward mannerisms. They are not so aggressive, blatant, outspoken. There are therefore many misunderstandings when Asian men come to the West. The new atmosphere of unisex among our younger generation, the fact that English girls can move with total freedom, go into pubs, have open friendships between male and female *without* any emotional involvement, leaves much ground for ambiguity of understanding. 'Just being friends' is an almost unknown concept in Asia between man and woman except among the minute proportion of sophisticated elite. Openhearted behaviour on the part of English women is therefore open to grave misunderstanding. So few Asian men have ever the chance to meet their own women on these natural terms, and can therefore hardly conceive of unemotional involvement based on purely social and mental equality of behaviour.

Caste

Caste at the village level in India is dying out very slowly. Within factories and town life the whole pattern of rigidity is breaking more quickly. The same piped water tap in a factory, for instance, has to be used by all for drinking purposes. Even the same goes for toilets. But it is beginning to show its strength again in the political arena because of the tussle for power and personal wealth at the village level where factions on caste lines have recently proved very strong. In the towns of Pakistan and India a new system of demarcation is appearing – between the well-placed and the displaced, marking the status of families as in Victorian England. This hinders the free matrimonial choice of partners, and social gatherings. In this respect Britain is now much more democratic in attitude and social workers have found great difficulty in understanding the rigidity of social hierarchy among the Asian communities of Britain. This needs to be recognised and brought out into the open. Many British women working as voluntary helpers treat the uneducated Asian women who come to the clinics with a greater sense of respect than do their own educated classes.

Health and Food

The Hindu is much influenced from the beginning by 'Ahimsa' – non-violence means non-killing. Respect for the life of all living creatures is deeply rooted in the Hindu mind. This is sometimes criticised by foreigners who raise the question of wars and the violence of partition between India and Pakistan.

Inevitably violence is part of human nature and the human condition but the Hindu will try, unless provoked or unless a higher duty or social code is endangered, to respect the idea of ahimsa. Killing for the sake of personal desire or satisfaction is forbidden. Therefore a great majority of orthodox Hindus eat no meat at all and are totally vegetarian to the extent even of refusing eggs as living matter, and onions as arousing passion and heating the blood, as well as because of the aesthetic sense that they smell on the breath, and cause intestinal wind.

The lack of meat certainly leads to dietary deficiencies in a cold climate where the vitamin D qualities of the life-giving sun are also absent. Yet another reason for rickets and TB appearing is that the browner Asian skin protects the inner fibre and cells of the body from absorbing too much sunlight. It is nature's own protection against radiation and ultra-violet rays in tropical climates. But where sun is lacking it even prevents the absorption of vitamin D from what little sun the British climate allows.

Also through lack of play outside and the fact that many Asian mothers do not venture out of doors too much, through unfamiliarity, psychological alienation and little English, children are very susceptible to respiratory diseases. Asian parents need much guidance in this respect as they do not understand how devastating the change of climate can be – living in an Asian village is an open-air life and, despite poverty, can be ironically healthier than crowded conditions in our slum areas.

Death

Hindus cremate the dead body (unlike Muslims who bury their dead in ancestral grounds and a very few Hindu sects who bury their dead in a cross-legged posture in salt). In India, of course, cremation is done matter of factly, in the open on high pyres of sweet-smelling sandalwood. The body is just wrapped in a simple cotton shroud, a few Sanskrit slokas are chanted and the ashes are collected, sometimes to be scattered in the holy river Ganges, known as Mother Ganges, or Ganga Ma, or at a centre of holy pilgrimage. Sometimes ashes are sent back from this country but on the whole, as death is accepted as a gateway to a new life, a renewal, in fact, the Hindu does not mind about particulars or ceremonies and has his ashes scattered naturally – in the words of the Brahmin: 'Yatraye tatre gachhte' – He goes to where he comes from.

The tradition of going to the Ganges on pilgrimage for religious reasons of cleansing the body and spirit is relevant to British authorities who may be seeking records of peoples births, marriages, and deaths. The majority of Hindu families at least will have recorded these with the family priests or pandas in the main holy cities. Family backgrounds – sometimes up to twenty generations and without mistakes – are recorded with the pandas even if civil authorities do not possess reliable documentation.

Names

The problem which the British generally face with the names of Indians and Pakistanis is well known. Too many Alis and Singhs have caused chaos in hospital and industrial and electoral records. The title Begum for instance is only a Muslim courtesy title for a woman. It is *not* a surname. All Sikh females use Kaur as a second name. It is *never* a surname. Registrars may be confused therefore if a Khuswant Singh comes to register his daughter as Mala Kaur. Neither Singh nor Kaur are surnames as we acknowledge them. Registrars and other authorities need to ask for a forename (not a 'Christian' name), a given name (often a pen name acquired in recent generations) or baptismal name, and a family or surname. Pakistani names have been dealt with in the section on Islam.

Among the Hindus traditions differ in different parts of the country – it is like travelling through Europe, so contrasting are the strong regional and cultural differences of India.

People with a fair complexion generally come from the Punjab and have a subcaste such as Puri, Sharwa, Kohli, Kapur, Khosla. This is used as the surname. The first name – corresponding to our Christian name – is often based on Sanskrit or the names of Hindu Gods and Goddesses or meanings of beautiful significance, certainly where girls' names are concerned. Purnima means 'night of full moon' and Kamal means 'Lotus-eyed'. Names such as Shiv, Krishen Mahesh, Arjun, Ram Kumar (son of Rama), Narayan all derive from the names of dieties and religious figures. Mostly the name consists of three parts:

Davinder Kumar Puri
Ajit Kumar Sharma.

Kumari means 'the daughter of', and is attached at the beginning of the name of a single girl such as Raj Kumari Amrit Kaur.

In Bengal Hindu names are in the same pattern but there are many more distinctive Sens, Boses, Tagores and Rays or Roys.

From Bombay side and Gujerat district as a rule the father's name and the professional title are included, as for example

Natha Lal	Bhiku Bhai	Patel
1	2	3

the first being the name of the individual, the second that of the father, the 'patel' standing for the agriculturalist, or the one who owns land. Mistry is another very familiar name for Gujeratis, meaning a mason or bricklayer, or a skilled person generally.

There are a few sects who use their religion as the surname – Mahesh Kumar *Jain*. And in South India the system is even more complicated. There are usually three names, and very elongated at that. Two brothers will have different names as surnames because in India these are their *personal* names which they use as surnames, dropping their caste names when they come here – and in the middle will be the village name – thus Sunderaraja Khottandaram Iyengar – will be using the first name as his proper name, the middle name for his village, the last name as his caste name. The last name may therefore be dropped and this person be known as Mr Sunderaraja. His brother may be Narasinha Kottandaram Iyengar and be known as Mr Narasinha.

Marathi names can often be picked out by the ending Kar, such as Mulgaokar, Karendikar, or Ambedkar. These people usually come from Bombay side.

ASIAN FESTIVALS

Political festivals

January 26*th*   Indian Republic Day

March 23*rd*   Pakistan Republic Day

August 14*th*   Independence Day.........Pakistan

August 15*th*   Independence Day.........India

(these two days celebrate the ending of the British Raj and the handing over of Independence to the two sovereign republics in 1947).

Religious and cultural festivals

January 18*th*   Sikh celebration of Guru Gobind Singh's birthday.

February 17*th* (1970)   The moveable Muslim commemoration of Ibrahim's offer

Eid-ul-Adha   to sacrifice his son, Ishmael, to the glory of God. Ibrahim's

(*or Zuha in*   family were in Mecca to look after the Holy place of the

Anglicised form)   Kaaba. This lunar date is commemorated a little earlier each year, working backwards through the Western calendar (see Islam section for full details). Goats and sheep are sacrificed and sold to raise money for orphanages and scholarships for the poor. This Eid concentrates the mind on the needs of poverty. Charitable institutions are set up with the money contributed. Families invite guests to dinner and there are huge congregational prayers in the mosques.

end February/March   *Basant* – another moveable date of the Indian Punjabi Spring festival when yellow turbans and saris and new long skirts (lehengaas, sometimes 15 yards at the hem) are donned. Yellow is the spring colour, reflected in the open plains of the Punjab in the sarson – the mustard-like vegetable which flames with yellow flowers. This is also the colour of bravery (just the opposite of the Western idiom), and fertility. This is the symbol of the yellow in the Indian flag going back to Rajput traditions. Fairs or melas are held and especially music concerts. There is a

Punjabi saying: 'Ai basant baleh urant' – when Basant comes, the cold flies away.

March 8th (1970)   *Muhurram* – a Muslim remembrance of the martyrdom of Hussain, Prophet Muhammed's grandson, especially celebrated by the Shia sect. The full explanation of Muhurram is in the section concerning Islam but it is interesting to note that it was on the tenth of Muhurram that Pharaoh and his army perished in the Nile waters while chasing Moses and his followers who were escaping across the Red Sea. In gratefulness for his deliverance Prophet Moses fasted on that day. So do the Jews now to commemorate this event and so did Muhammed enjoin Muslims to fast both on the tenth day but also on the ninth or eleventh day as well, so carrying on the Semetic tradition.

Shrines or Imambaras of Muslim Saints are illuminated at night in Pakistan, and also in India.

Forty years after the death of Muhammed (during the Caliphate of Yazid) Hussain was killed on the same day. All Muslims recite the Quran at the beginning of this month for the good of his departed soul. The Shia sect who take their descendancy from Hussain, mourn his death for forty days. Meetings are held in the evenings for the first nine days to recall the incidents of his life for the benefit of the younger generation and a mourning procession is taken out on the tenth day, while chanting of religious hymns, ballads and the flagellation of some of the more fervent members of the crowd accompany the great *tazias* or floats of Hussain, and the bamboo replicas of the martyr's tomb at Karbala in modern Iraq.

circa March   *Holi* – the Hindu festival, a Bacchanalia of fertility and spring, celebrated in Northern and Central India but not in Bengal or the South. It goes back to very ancient times to the mythology of the cruel King, Harna Kashyap, and his step-son Prahlad whom he hated because he was very religious. One day he decided to kill Prahlad for worshipping the Divine, instead of himself – and tried to enlist the help of his sister, Holika. She had been blessed by the Devas and could not be touched by fire, so that when Kashyap lit a bonfire to destroy Prahlad (whom he had sat on Holika's lap in the bonfire), Holika was burnt up and Prahlad escaped, untouched by the flames. Hindus now celebrate this as one more triumph of the forces of Good over Evil.

Symbolically it is the Indian harvest thanksgiving in a country-side which can support three crops a year if properly tilled. The spring wheat and ravi are harvested at this time and there is much singing and merry-making.

The throwing of red powder and water over anyone in sight up to midday of Holi expresses the intoxication and lack of inhibition similar to the Mardi Gras of Latin countries before Lent, and the Greek Dionysian rites. By the orthodox Hindu calendar the Lord Krishna returns on this day to Gokul, the temple city of Brindaban, near Delhi, playing his flute and dancing with the Gopis or milkmaids. One of the cow-herds dancing for joy smeared the Gopis with turmeric powder mixed in milk so in turn they took kum-kum powder (the red decorative cosmetic powder) and sprinkled it on the men.

Nowadays it is a day for wild childish pranks.

April 13*th*   *Baisakhi* – the first day of the Sikh and Hindu New Year commemorating the founding of the Khalsa, the society of the pure. In several parts of Northern India it heralds the advent of a new fiscal year. To the masses it means the beginning of the new Bikrami Samiti, and to the farmer rewards for the winter toil.

To Indians in general and to Punjabis in particular it brings back memories of the dark day of Jallianwala Bagh when General Dwyer's troops fired on a crowd of Indian freedom fighters gathered in this enclosed square in Amritsar. Since that day this festival has also been re-membered as Martyrs Day.

For the Sikhs this day has special significance. Guru Amar Das – the third Guru – made it one of the annual gatherings of the Sikhs, the other being Diwali, so that the Sikhs would retain their own celebrations rather than Hindu ones at the time when the Sikh religion was still in its infancy.

There is much festivity in Punjabi villages, melas, cattle contests in drawing the Persian wheel, and bhangra dancing where young Sikh men dance on an upturned gharra or earthenware pot *on top of* another Sikh's head.

May 18*th* (1970)   Eid-milad-un-Nabi, Prophet Muhammed's birthday.

May 21*st* (1970)   *Buddha Purnima* – Celebration of the birth of the Lord Buddha more than 2,500 years ago.

July-August   *Raksha Bandan* – A secular Indian ceremony. However it traces its ancestry back to Hindu mythological beginnings.

It falls on the full moon day of the Indian summer month of Shravan. Raksha means 'to protect' and bandhan means 'to tie'.

The legend goes that when Indra, the Vedic God of the

85

Heavens, was defeated in an encounter with Bali the Demon King, Indra's wife asked the Lord Vishnu for help. The God gave her a thread invested with supernatural powers to tie on the wrist of Indra. This amulet protected Indra and gave him added strength to defeat Bali.

Nowadays further layers of history have been added to the occasion when sisters and mothers tie a band around their menfolk, especially brothers (girls can 'adopt brothers' from males outside the family), with the prayer that they may be protected from all evil by the tieing on the wrist of multi-coloured tinselled rakhis. These are now sold in Indian shops in this country for the occasion.

After taking a bath in the morning the whole family assembles in decorated homes and the following is said as the sister ties the band.

> 'That thread by which Indra tied down the great, strong demon-king Bali; Oh, brother, with that I tie thee to protect you from all evils. Oh, amulet, may you not fail; may you not fail.'

Even in the days of Moghul rule, like much else in India, Muslim and Hindu culture was fused into a common Indian culture of synthesis and Hindu Rajput queens of the sixteenth and seventeenth centuries sent rakhis to Muslim rulers when their own husbands were away fighting neighbouring rulers or marauding invaders. The Rani of Mewar is famous for sending such an amulet to the Muslim Emperor Humayan when threatened with an armed attack. Humayan understood the significance of this and sent immediate help to the Rani.

circa end August   *Janmashtami* – The Nativity Festival of Lord Krishna. This is held on the eighth day of the dark part of the month during the lunar waning. His birth place was the prison of a tyrant and legend has it that (like the birth of Moses) he was rescued from prison by the swopping of babies.

The Lord Krishna – the 'Blue God' – is symbolic of too much to the average Indian whether he is Hindu or not. He is perhaps most the symbol of the eternal God who drinks the whole poison of evil in the universe which turned him this colour to protect mankind from such evil. In Sanskrit it is said: 'Karshti sai Krishn' – 'That who attracts is Krishna'. A myriad legends are woven around this incarnation of the Lord Vishnu. He is the child Krishna who plays naughty pranks on everyone, and the amorous lover, the Hindu Cupid who steals the clothes of the Gopis while they are bathing in the river Jumna; he is the heroic warrior and philosopher of the epic Mahabharata; he is the diplomat who always championed the cause of justice; he epitomises to orthodox Hindus the social and ethical values embedded in their long philosophical scriptures. He is above all, beloved, not being remote or ascetic like Vishnu or Shiva. Usually he is depicted wandering in the mystic woods playing glorious melodies from his ever-present flute.

One of the most famous legends based on historical fact is that of Krishna plunging into the waters of the Jumna near Mathura, south of Delhi, to fight the Kalinag (the Black Snake) representative of the Naga system of life which was very prevalent in those days (a thousand years before the Christian era). The whole story personifies the struggle for dominance at that time of the Hindu culture over the Hoon and Naga savages who lived outside the Hindu system. Krishna plunges into the waters and the Kalinag (the only time a serpent appears in an evil light in Hindu mythology) ejects the dark venom to fight Krishna who is also the embodiment of the six main philosophies of Hinduism which are finally amalgamated and made whole in the Bhagavad Gita – the Song of the Lord, expounded by Krishna.

Krishna emerges from the turbulent waters standing on the head of Kalinag and holding in rein the six heads (again symbolising the six systems of thought) of the serpent.

Janamashtami or Krishanashtami falls at midnight, the time of the birth. It is celebrated mainly in North and Central India, and especially by the Gujerati Patels and the Maharashtrians from Bombay side who have come to Britain. Small devas of the Lord Krishna are on many English mantelpieces in this country. Back in India men and women fast on the previous day and after the birth time they eat sweetmeats after first offering them to the image of God. Usually they do this in the temple where they spent the whole night singing Kirtans and bhajans till midnight. Then they place the image of the baby Krishna in a flower-bedecked cradle and all night they celebrate his birth.

September/October   *Ram Navami* – The ninth day of the fight between the historical King Rama of Ayodhya, and Ravan, the Demon King of Lanka (Ceylon).

October   *Dussehra* – Again of unfixed date depending on the full moon. This, one of the greatest Hindu festivals celebrated universally by all Indians, follows immediately upon Ramnavami and is described in the Hinduism section.

It is terminated after 10 days of enactment of the Rama-Sita epic on open maidans by the autumn Festival of Lights.

Beginning November *Diwali or Deepawali* – The Hindu festival symbolic again of the forces of good over evil. On this dark night the Goddess Lakshmi, personification of good Fortune and Prosperity, visits only those homes that are lit by the lights of many lamps – usually the saucer-shaped earthenware deepas filled with coconut oil and rolled cotton wicks. Woe betide the house enshrouded in darkness. This is a beautiful festival with houses and humble mud huts alike flickering in the light of thousands of such lamps.

This is also the day when a majority of business communities terminate the fiscal year and open new ledgers on the morning after Diwali. It also commemorated the welcome home to Rama after 14 years of exile and his coronation as the King of the Northern Kingdom of Ayodhya.

October/November *Durga Puja* – is the Bengali Festival in honour of the Goddess Durga, the female principle of Energy and earth fertility, the Mother to be revered, the saviour (Durg means castle in Sanskrit) who protects you from external dangers just as the fortress castle does.

End November/ *Guru Nanak's Birthday*, the founder of the Sikh faith and
beginning December the first of the ten Gurus. This birth day is fixed again according to the lunar month. In 1969, the 500th anniversary of the Guru's birth in 1469, the day fell on November 23.

November *Ramadan* (sometimes spelt Ramazaan). In 1970 this full month of fasting will fall in the whole of November to culminate in the Eid-ul-Fitr.

End November *Eid-ul-Fitr*, the great day of feasting when Muslims the world over break their strenuous discipline of fasting from sunrise to sunset for four long weeks. On this day special spiced dishes are cooked, decorations are hung as at the Christian Christmas, and families reunite and have a gay time. Each year following this commemoration the Festival will fall approximately 10-11 days earlier in the Roman calendar.